THE CIVILIZATION OF
ISLAM

THE CIVILIZATION OF
ISLAM

Text by
Jean Mathé
Translated by David Macrae

Crescent Books
New York

CONTENTS :

Introduction 5
1. Islamic Society 19
2. The Muslim Family 31
3. Home and Daily Life 49
4. Resources and Work 77
5. Sciences, Literature and Arts . . 119
6. The Islamic Faith 153
Chronologies 172

First English edition published by
Editions Minerva S.A., Genève.
Copyright © MCMLXXX
Editions Minerva S.A., Genève.
All rights reserved.

Library of Congress Catalog Card
Number: 79-57034
ISBN: 0-517-307057

This edition is published by Crescent Books,
a division of Crown Publishers, Inc.

a b c d e f g h
Printed in Italy

INTRODUCTION

Pre-Islamic Arabia

The Arabian peninsula, the cradle of Islam, is the geological continuation of the Sahara which is prolonged, across the Iranian Plateau, as far as the Gobi Desert.

The fractures of the Red Sea and the Persian Gulf served merely to heighten its isolation and accentuate even more strongly the merciless grip which the desert environment has always had on those who had to struggle for their survival there.

The peninsula, which has been inhabited since the earliest times despite the harsh living conditions which it offered, was the great closed preserve of the Semitic tribes; in fact it was named the Island of the Arabs.

These Arabs, whose name was already used by the Assyrian chroniclers, found in this region an ideal world for the emergence of their immutable characteristics—unstable independence and fitful courage.

In the pre-Islamic period the bulk of the population consisted of the tribes of Bedouin whose nomadic mode of life was the best possible way to adapt to the grim living conditions they had to face. These Bedouins are thus the original quintessence of the Arabs. Yet a small minority of merchants founded the only towns in the country: Yathrib (Medina) and Mecca in the Hejaz. The exception here is the superbly lush oases of Yemen, miraculously irrigated by the tip of a monsoon which fertilizes them to such an extent that they came to be known as Arabia Felix.

Everyone lived exclusively off the caravan trade which criss-crossed the desert, linking the peninsulà to its rich neighbors: Petra, Damascus, Palmyra and Persia.

In this forbidding environment the religious development of the Arabs did not reach a high level: a naive paganism, with ill-defined divinities borrowed from other polytheistic religions—Allat, the goddess of the sun; Manat, the goddess of bad luck, or Wadd, the god of love.

In addition to these there were numerous local idols, good and evil spirits, and a naturalistic worship of rocks, trees and springs.

These loosely related pagan beliefs were, however, strong enough even at this early stage to sustain the pilgrimage to Mecca, where believers flocked to adore a strange cube draped in black, the Kaaba.

According to legend it had been raised by Adam, destroyed by the Flood, and rebuilt by Abraham with the help of his son Ishmael, father of all the Arabs.

A legendary black stone is sealed into a corner of the building; it is supposed to have fallen from Paradise and been brought to the Patriarch by the Archangel Gabriel (Djebrail) during the reconstruction of the Temple.

Amongst this medley of pagan and fetishist beliefs which preceded the burgeoning of Islam, the name of Allah was merely that of a local divinity venerated in the Kaaba. Meanwhile, the influence of the two great monotheist religions was beginning to infiltrate into the peninsula: the Jews, who were already highly organized in tribes, were the active minority of the merchants of Mecca, while Christianity, which was present only very superficially, did no more than provide an additional form of fetishism in the oases, with a profusion of small ivory crosses.

Mohammed

Little is known about the life of the Prophet; such knowledge as we have derives solely from the Koran, tradition or a number of chronicles which were more or less embroidered by his disciples.

It is thought that he was born in 570 in Mecca, the son of a merchant who died before his birth; his mother died a few years later. According to tradition he was raised by his paternal uncle, Abu Talib. He grew up with his young cousin Ali, who was to become one of his most faithful companions and disciples and, later on, his son-in-law.

Until the age of forty it seems that he lived without any particular mystical preoccupation, going with his uncle on his travels, and marrying his first wife, Khadija, about the age of twenty.

Then, all of a sudden, on the twenty-sixth day of the month of Ramadan in the year 610, his religious crisis began: he had visions and heard voices urging him to preach the exclusive monotheism of Allah, who had now been elevated to the rank of sole, universal and absolute God.

This new religion, as thus revealed, provided him with the substance of the Koran and of his divinely inspired preaching, which began at Mecca in 613. At first it was very poorly received by the conservative, profit-minded Arab merchants

whose habits of money-making and rivalry were thus upset. On the other hand it seems to have met with a more favorable response on the part of the most disadvantaged Bedouins, to whom it brought hope of divine justice and the compensation of resurrection.

The ideas of monotheism were clearly in men's minds in the Middle East and had already become crystallized in the two major neighboring religions. Moreover a reform-minded Arab minority, the Hanifs, tired of the selfish behavior of the merchants, opposed to the infiltration of Judaism, and distressed by the anarchy of an ineffective, decadent and haphazard paganism, represented a vague aspiration for an ideal of justice and purifying mysticism.

The opposition eventually prevailed; and Mohammed, having lost his uncle and his wife, decided in 622 to leave Mecca for Medina.

This voluntary exile was the *Hegira,* the point of departure of the Moslem calendar and the date of birth of militant Islam.

All was not simple, despite the more sympathetic reception extended to him and the establishment of a first nucleus of faithful followers. There were in Medina three Jewish tribes which controlled most of the trade in the city. The Rabbis ridiculed the Prophet and perscuted him unrelentingly.

Mohammed than realized that he had to impose his nascent Islam by force and confer upon his still unsteady religion the baptism of fire, before it became choked to death by a combination of the as yet disunited opposing forces.

In 624 he sent his first groups of mystic fighters into action against his opponents, who had regrouped at Badr, on the Hejaz coast, and crushed them.

This victory established his authority and enabled him to eliminate some of the Jewish groups in the city. The same thing happened again in 625. Mecca, now thoroughly alarmed, went to war against the Prophet of Medina. The two cities clashed. The victorious Prophet then made his triumphant entry into his native city. The ordinary people who, in their superstition, were ready to see the divine intervention in any human achievement, were convinced that the Prophet was endowed with supernatural powers.

Thenceforth the spiritual master of Arabia, the Prophet denounced the pagan cult of the Kaaba. He had its doors opened, smashed its idols and proclaimed the single and universal reign of Allah.

Yet he remained as moderate and magnanimous in triumph as he had been tough and intransigent in battle. He chose not to upset the ancestral customs of the Arabs and merely imposed on them the strict moral rules of a monotheism which was demanding but, at the same time, politically merciful.

This took place in 630, the 8th year of the Hegira: there were only two years left for Mohammed to consolidate his life's work before dying.

The last of the hostile Bedouins rallied to his cause, the remaining merchants, in fear, quickly became converted and the Jews were expelled. Medina was confirmed as the capital of Islam.

At the age of 61 on 8 June 632, Mohammed died after an unidentified illness lasting several days, on his return from a final pilgrimage to Mecca, only a few months before his only son Ibrahim.

He left a daughter, Fatima, and a son-in-law, Ali. But he left no appointed successor and no political or religious testament.

He had merely sketched out the main outlines of his plans, and no one can say which way Islam would have gone if he had lived.

The succession to Mohammed: the first Caliphs

Suddenly confronted with the need to find a successor to the Master, the Prophet's companions improvised by creating the post of the caliph, who was to be the vicar and lieutenant of Allah on earth.

Omar the Wise decided against Ali, the son-in-law of the Prophet, and in favor of Abu-Bek, the oldest and most deeply venerated of the companions of Mohammed.

Thereupon began the expansionist raids of conquest on behalf of Islam and Arabism.

Attacking in small groups of a few thousand men, the Bedouin, lacking in technique and strategy but driven by an irresistible mystical enthusiasm, defeated the Byzantines and the Sassanids of Persia.

Their expansion took place with the speed of lightning: Damascus fell in 635, Jerusalem in 638, and Caesarea in 640.

The Bedouins made surprise attacks in veritable whirlwinds of crazed courage and exuberant fanaticism—not unlike the shock troops of Lawrence of Arabia centuries later. These soldiers of Allah were headed by an improvised general, Khalib, known as the Sword of Islam on account of his remarkable vigor and ability.

Abu-Bekr died in 634, after two years of a reign marked by external expansion and wise domestic policies.

Omar succeeded him after the orthodox faction, which continued to support Ali, had been defeated in the power struggle.

Then followed ten years of a caliphate of exemplary intelligence and lucidity. Having been the Prophet's right-hand man since the Hegira, he at first continued the expansion of a victorious Islam. Tough yet pious, inflexible yet human, he kept a firm and uncompromising grip on the new religion and the new empire, steering both along the path of rigor. At one point he did not hesitate to criticize Khalib, the

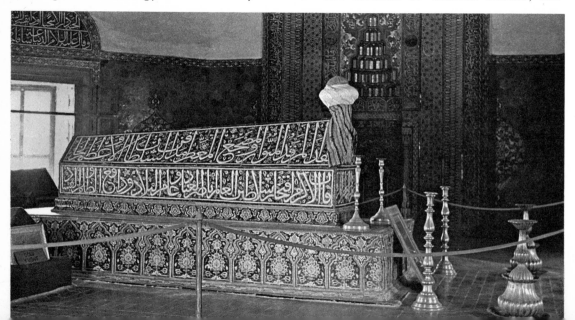

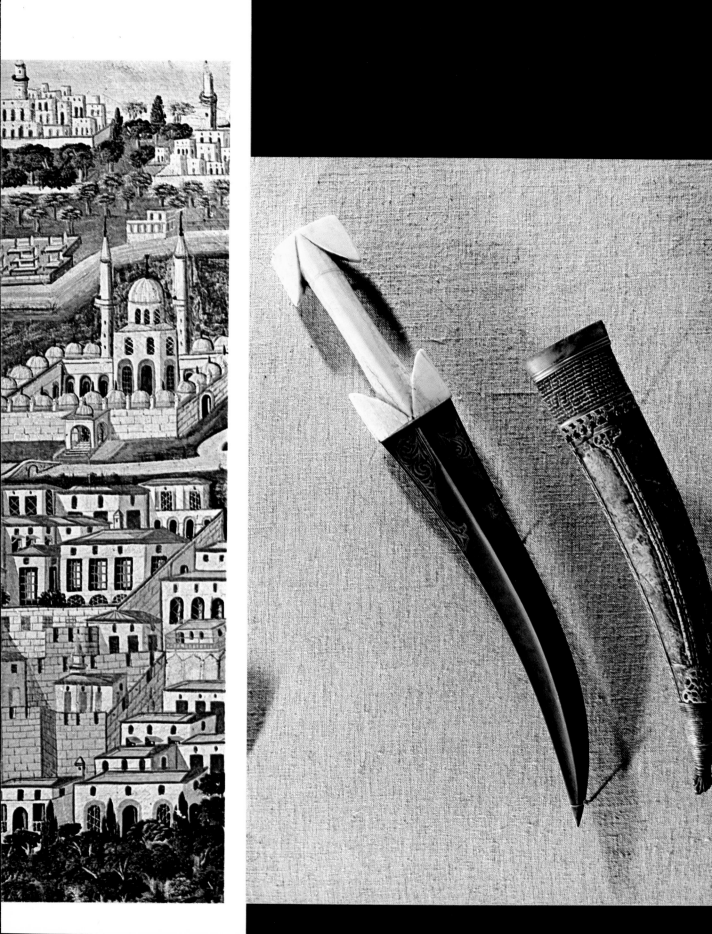

Sword of Allah, who was actually a national hero, because he had committed acts of cruelty which could harm the image of the new religion in the conquered areas.

He was assassinated in 644, at the age of 63. The official version holds that he was killed by a Christian slave over some minor tax problem; though his death may well have been the result of a plot by Muslim leaders who were disturbed by the caliph's virtuous rigor, which was increasingly bad for their interests.

In the military sphere he had had the time to complete the conquest of Iran, Egypt, Syria and Irak, thus bringing to a close the first wave of politico-religious territorial expansion.

Once again the council of notables chose not to confer the caliphate on Ali; instead they turned to Othman who, though pious, honest and sincere, was weak and easily led.

This was too much for the orthodox faction which supported Ali and Fatima, and their opposition was then declared openly. There was certainly no shortage of pretexts. The rich Banu-Umayya merchants of Damascus, although they had remained pagan until a very late date and were the last to become converted, already held the key posts. Moreover, they violated the Koranic Law which made it illegal for an Arab to own land outside the Arabian peninsula: in order to secure the support of the military and the notables they rewarded them with land grants from the conquered and occupied territories.

In a rage, the orthodox Bedouin converged from the provinces towards Medina. The Egyptians, who arrived first, assassinated Othman. Ali, who had probably stirred up this conflict, finally acceded to the caliphate in 656, whereupon he moved his capital to Kufa, in Irak, far from the corruption of Damascus.

But the tribe of the Banu-Umayya, the Omayyads of Damascus to whom Othman

had belonged, challenged the new caliph, accusing him of arranging the deadly conspiracy, and marched on Kufa. A civil war then took place between the two religious clans. The rebellious Omayyads clashed with the orthodox supporters of Ali at Siffin, in Irak.

In order to avoid further bloodshed between Muslims, the Prophet's son-in-law agreed—unwisely, as it turned out—to accept arbitration. The biased ruling went in favor of the Banu-Umayya, making their leader, Muawiya, the new caliph.

In 657, therefore, the situation was inextricable: in Damascus there was an official caliph, the Omayyad Muawiya, who was opposed by the ousted caliph, Ali, the Prophet's son-in-law, who was based in Kufa.

This imbroglio was further complicated by the murderous raids of the Kharijites, a group of tough anarchistic Puritans who rejected all religious hierarchies of whatever leaning, and favored a democratic, almost a "socialist" Islam.

These raids took the form of outbursts of fanatical and destructive rage. It was the sword of a Kharijite that killed Ali in the mosque at Kufa in January 661, thus turning his failure into a martyrdom. Though strongly opposed during his lifetime, he became sanctified by death. This marked the beginning of the great schism which still divides Islam: the Sunnites who accept the authority of all the elected caliphs, and the Shiites who recognize only the brief dynasty of the direct descendants of the Prophet: Ali, Fatima and their son Hussein.

The Omayyads

In the family of the Banu-Umayya, Muawiya founded a brilliant dynasty which was to occupy the caliphate for ninety years.

This was to be the most prosperous and homogeneous century in the whole of the history of Islam.

As the Omayyads had become converted forcibly and very late, their faith was not

Right: Muslim soldiers attacking a fortified town: note the military hardware with which they are equipped. By the use of flaming naphtha the Islamic warriors terrorized the enemy cavalry. Bottom: the fortifications of a city.

quite fanatical, though its sincerity was never in doubt. The religious element was therefore not of exclusive or even of prime importance for their state. The caliphate, which had previously been purely sacred and patriarchal, became political, and gradually evolved into a genuine monarchy with absolutist tendencies.

While struggling first against the violence of the Kharijites and opposition of the orthodox Shiites represented by the Abbasids of Irak, they built a powerful and relatively unitary state.

The era of the great conquests could then resume. But this time the driving force behind the fighters in this holy war was quite as much Arabism and a thirst for territorial expansion as a mission to spread Islam throughout the world.

The Omayyad conquests were above all a quest for broad Arab hegemony, both political and economic, from the Mediterranean to the Far East. This is made particularly evident by the fact that they did not even make the vanquished peoples convert to Islam, and merely obliged them, if they wanted to remain 'infidels', to pay taxes and levies.

These territorial annexations were remarkable for their terrifying rapidity.

In the East, the Indus, Merv and Samarkand were reached in 712.

In the West, the whole of North Africa was conquered between 700 and 709, despite the fierce resistance of the Berbers, a people related to the Bedouin which soon, however, became Islamicized and took part in the conquest of Spain. This latter venture began in 712 and was virtually complete by the end of 713, leaving the 'Spanish' themselves holding only the north-west corner of the peninsula. The Pyrenees were crossed in 718; in 732 Bordeaux and Tours were occupied. But at Poitiers Charles Martel barred any further advance by the forces of Abd-er-Rahman. Now far from their bases, and relying on lightning raids with no real strategic occupation of the area, the Arabs had finally reached the extreme limit of their advance.

Meanwhile, however, the remote central authority of Damascus was softening and beginning to crumble.

There was a rekindling of dissent, deriving from the Iranian Khorassan and encouraged by the orthodox Shiites. In 750 the last of the Omayyad caliphs was overthrown in a full-scale revolution, directly contrary to that of 657, and an Abassid of Baghdad mounted the throne of the successors of Mohammed.

The Abassids

They took their name from Abbas, the uncle of Mohammed. They were pure orthodox, recognizing only the spiritual authority of the descendants of the Prophet.

Their country was Irak and Iran, and their capital Baghdad; they contemptuously ignored Damascus, which they regarded as a superficial and corrupt city. For them all that mattered was Islam, its exalted propaganda, and the intransigent dissemination of the Koran.

Arabism, which had once been a major concern of theirs, now ceased to have any importance at all. Gradually the notion of the supra-nationality of religion led to a dislocation of the political state. The highest offices were not even reserved for Arabs. 'Foreigners', having been conquered and then Islamicized, thenceforth had access to posts of responsibility: Turks, Berbers, Spaniard, Egyptians, Iranians infiltrated the system, fed on it like parasites and prevented it from working.

The result was a gradual disappearance of central power and the collapse of the politically fragmented empire.

Provincial caliphates were created in each territory: with the passage of time they declared themselves independent of Baghdad, which took no action against them.

Tunisia and Morocco seceded in 788, Spain in 756 and Egypt in 869.

Within a few years, Irak alone represented the purely Arab Islam of the Abassids.

This was the age of Al Mansur and Harum-er-Rashid. The eighth and ninth centuries were the apogee of the Baghdad of the Thousand and One Nights. The prestige of this glittering capital was the envy of the entire Orient.

Its radiance, however, was religious and artistic rather than political, as the central authority of the Empire had faded and no longer extended to the remoter conquered territories.

Decadence and collapse

The abandonment of political pan-Arabism by the central authority gradually relegated the caliphate to an honorary spiritual function, not unlike that of our modern papacy.

The title "caliph", which had previously been reserved for Arabs and used with reference to a single elevated office, now became downgraded. 'Foreigners' could now be caliphs; each rich city wanted a caliphate of its own. Granada, Cordova, Seville, for example, vied with each other for supremacy in Spain.

This weakening and disintegration made the Empire an easy prey for each succeeding wave of invaders, bringing an endless flow of peoples anxious to carve out their own piece of territory or of opponents of Islam seeking to restore their endangered religions.

In the tenth and eleventh centuries the Seljucid Turks; from the eleventh to the thirteenth centuries the Crusaders; in the thirteenth and fourteenth centuries the Mongols, the Timurids of Tamerlane, who devastated Iran in the fifteenth century, while the Mamelukes supplanted the Ottomans in Turkey and Egypt.

There was no longer any Islamic Arab Empire: the last of the elected caliphs of Baghdad was killed by the Mongol hordes of Hulagu.

Then the last caliphate in Europe disappeared in 1492, when the Christian 're-conquest' drove Boabdil out of Granada.

From then on, Islam was only a religion separated from the political power of states. Yet it still had astonishing vitality and a fantastic ability to spread throughout the world.

Modern Islam—Islam and us

However, in all countries which had once had commercial contact with the Arabs, Islam exploded and spread, covering India, Africa and Asia.

The religious force of its faith and the power of its inspired mystical fanaticism overcame errors, quarrels and political selfishness.

Despite an age of acute nationalism and economic rivalries which had destroyed the dream of Arab unity, the faith of Allah continued to win converts.

In fact one wonders whether Islam, which now has more than 500 million faithful, is a religion, a philosophy or a social order.

In any case, now that the Arab world, having slept for centuries, has awoken and returned to the forefront of international affairs, our Western civilizations are incredulous and amazed. They had grown accustomed to taking a disdainful or condescending view of the Arabs.

I — ISLAMIC SOCIETY

At the dawn of Islam, Arabia, which was isolated from the rest of the world by seas, climate and deserts, was both a prison and a refuge for the Bedouins, the original ethnic component of the Arabs. They represented the southern branch of the Semites just as the Hebrews, Phenicians, Arameans and Chaldeans, who had already emigrated towards their places of definitive settlement, were its northern branch.

Even within the Arab ethnic entity, there was another profound division, between the 'northerners' of Arabia, the sons of Qahtan, and the Yemenite 'southerners', the sons of Adnan.

Traditionally these two groups had been violently opposed to each other, each claiming to be the only one linked to the Biblical epic and the offspring of Ishmael.

Yet, regardless of the nature of such conflict and rancor, they counted for little in the daily practice of survival, since the Arabian peninsula had, for thousands of years, been the setting for the merciless civilization of the desert.

The pillars of that primitive society were immutable: grass, camel and tribe.

In order to survive it was necessary to keep on the move, following the lifegiving grass wherever it might be, since it alone enabled the Bedouin to sustain the flock which provided the milk, meat, wool and hides needed for a small-scale family-based economy.

Movement was therefore the key to Bedouin life. However, in order to move about the desert an animal was necessary: the providential dromadary.

This creature, which first made its appearance early in the second millenium BC, revolutionized Arab life. Henceforth it

The tribes settle for the most part in arid desert areas, where they build houses which are particularly well adapted to the climatic conditions.

became possible to transport whole camps, complete with the characteristic black tents, to wherever a chance shower had generated a short-lived pasture. The steady and powerful dromadary is capable of carrying loads of more than six hundred pounds over more than two hundred miles of desert. It carried along, swaying gently from side to side, the palanquins of the Arab women, the vast tents made of goat's hair, the sacks of grain without which it would be impossible to maintain the horses or the few lean hens which provided a small number of extremely welcome eggs.

The horse was the pride of the Bedouin, and the impetuous companion of the warrior. Another, less noble side of its character was the role it played in the raids which were an inseparable part of desert life. Such marauding was allowed as a sport, a legitimate means of exacting vengeance, and as a valuable source of profit in the form of booty.

In this inferno of blazing hot sand, wells were essential to the survival of men and animals. The position of these pathetic holes in the ground, only a few yards wide, was a part of the knowledge passed down from one generation to the next. It was something of a miracle that they could be found at all in such a featureless landscape, but they were tirelessly cleared of sand each time they became covered in drifts. The water they provided was for the most part muddy and brackish, yet the nomadic Bedouin eagerly plunged their characteristic goatskin flasks into this life-giving liquid.

Family and tribe

The basis of this society, whether settled or wandering, was the family, solidly clustered around the father, who was the absolute and undisputed head. Yet the true social structure of the Bedouin was the association of several families in a tribe.

At its head there was a sheikh, appointed by the heads of the families. He wielded his authority over the small community, aided by a council of the wisest patriarchs. This authority was, however, accepted and recognized only on the absolute condition that ancestral tradition, a kind of code of honor, was respected.

Tribal pride was immensely strong, and was the origin of the endless raids and tribal wars on which the sheikhs decided to embark. The truth of the matter was that no one could possibly survive in such a hostile world outside the group. Unless one belonged to a clan, one could not feed one's flocks on collective pastures, nor marry one's daughters, nor exchange or acquire the necessities of life, nor even use the wells or the sacred sanctuaries which dispensed the favor of the gods.

Anyone who was marginal, independent or excluded from this group was doomed.

Structures

In this nomadic life there were very few anchorages: the pagan and fetishist temples and the markets situated in the sedentary oases.

It was there that the Bedouin—merchants and livestock-breeders—provided their nomadic brothers with grain, weapons and the prime necessities of life, in exchange for cattle or carpets.

Socially the cities and markets were merely fixed tribes, as ritual and traditions remained the same in them. Trade, moreover, grew from the combination of itinerants and settlement-dwellers, forming a complementary economic chain with an identical social structure.

The coming of Mohammed and Islam certainly entailed a constraint which the Bedouin took a long time to accept; in return, however, they were given hope of justice and the promise of compensation, in the world to come, for the day-to-day hardships of their lives.

With their hot-headed temperament and extreme distaste for all central authority, the Arabs rejected any organization which went beyond the tribal framework.

Independent, tough and dignified, yet friendly and faithful to their commitments, they represented a sort of idealistic chivalry, being by vocation nomadic shepherds, by instinct impulsive warriors and out of necessity aggressive in the defense of their only moral or material wealth.

After the initial turbulence, the Bedouin proved to be the best supporters of Mohammed in the establishment of Islam against the selfish merchants and the best of his fighters for the cause of Muslim pan-Arabism.

Living in a barren and austere world, the Bedouin had few needs but many rites. Though quick to engage in plunder and murder—which were regarded as the normal accidents of their fanatical exuberance—they were also capable of unselfish magnanimity, sweeping acts of generosity and of refined hospitality.

Had it not been for Mohammed and Islam, they would probably have vegetated for centuries in their deserts.

What Mohammed provided was not so much an upheaval or a revelation, as the gradual and prudent organization and then the expansion of Islamic vitality.

Being too respectful towards tradition to make innovations, they were content to merely improvise a central authority of a highly pragmatic nature.

This did not yet constitute a state: it was nothing more than a kind of civil code which complemented the precepts revealed by the Koran in order to unify the people and mobilize it towards one single goal: the expansion of Arabism, and Islam, its faith.

This 'holy war' of conquest contained and legalized the popular urge for violence, while giving it a basis, a mystical motiv-

ation, and, at the same time, offering hope for success.

The first Mohammedan society was based on a common faith and on the fulfilment of individual rights and duties. This attempt to achieve unity and equality —something quite revolutionary for the Arabs of that period—has often been referred to as a kind of Islamic socialism.

The arrangements devised by the Prophet, who had been promoted to the rank of head of state of Medina, were really day-to-day decisions. These spontaneous acts which, after the Prophet's death came to constitute a kind of jurisprudence for the purists of Islam, were often merely improvised solutions adopted in response to unforeseen situations.

The Prophet did not live long enough for us to have any idea as to how he really intended the temporal state born of his spiritual revolution to develop.

This was the responsibility of the caliphs who succeeded him. The military expansion of Islam through conquest was among their chief aims. In this way, the fiery Bedouin galloping towards the Mediterranean or the Indus were originally to a very great extent the conquering soldiers of Allah and Mohammed.

Omar was the only one who foresaw this urgent need for an administrative, political and economic structure to support and sustain this mystical explosion.

However, it was the Omayyads of Damascus who, having held the caliphate for a whole century, enlarged upon his ideas, and set up one of the most impressive and efficient power structures since the great cities of antiquity.

Arab hegemony then extended over the territory of Alexander's empire, and the

southern part of the Roman world. Needless to say, a solid homogeneous structure was essential if power was not be dissipated over so many remote, diverse and even contending provinces.

The caliph, the master of the Empire, usually came from one single family. Ancestral power was thus dynastic in nature.

The society over which he truly reigned, as both spiritual leader and head of state, consisted of several very different classes.

First there were the great tribal families, the Companions of the Prophet, and the Arabs converted to Islam from the beginning. They proved reliable administrators and soldiers of conquest.

There were also the late converts, those who had accepted Islam through obligation, self-interest, delayed conviction or convenience: this was true of the great mass of the conquered peoples, seeking to become integrated with the new source of power.

And there were also the "infidels", towards whom the policy of Islam was one of biased tolerance. They were the pagans or fetishists expelled from the territories controlled by the Arabs. But believers in one of the two other great revealed religions, Judaism or Christianity, found themselves not only admitted but also protected by their conquerors, in return for the payment of a tax.

Last came the slaves, who were left out of everything, but were exploited by all.

As soon as a territory was conquered, the caliph established his administration.

Administration

The key post was that of vizir, a kind of prime minister appointed by the caliph. Often chosen from the same family, the vizirs constituted a dynasty of high office holders. The caliphs had a firm grip on the central executive power: major decisions on domestic and foreign policies were their exclusive province, and they also had considerable spiritual power.

During the Omayyad century, they were of course exclusively Arabs, as the state was concerned quite as much with the hegemony of Arabism as the spread of Islam. The saber of Allah was mainly busy carving out new territories for Allah rather than new fields for conversion.

The vizirs, in particular, were more concerned with politics than with religion.

The extent of their powers made secession from the remote central authority of their caliph both easy and tempting.

In the period during which the vizirs were Arabs and the caliphs powerful, cohesion was maintained. But from the Abassid period onwards the deterioration of central authority and doctrinal laxity made it possible for 'foreigners'—Muslims but not Arabs—to become vizirs. A succession of Egyptians, Turkish and converted Spaniards then occupied this highest post: administrative breakdown then followed, and the provinces gradually recovered their autonomy.

It is to be noted that the conquerors never forced the vanquished peoples to convert to Islam, requiring of them merely their administrative allegiance and the payment of taxes.

Moreover, apart from the esteem felt by Mohammed and his successors for the two other monotheistic religions, the number of non-Muslims was too great and their economic role too essential for the idea of eliminating them ever to be taken seriously. The finances and business of the conquered lands were in their hands: there were 500,000 Christians in Irak and two million in Egypt, while there were 600,000 Jews in Irak and one million in Iran.

They were therefore allowed to remain where they were and even to keep their property and businesses, in return for the payment of special taxes. Omar was responsible for setting up this administrative structure. The governor was assisted by two officials, appointed by the caliph, who wielded immense power in their provinces, where they represented the temporal extension of the central authority. They were the *amil,* a financial delegate, and the *wali,* or military governor. After all, the army and taxation were the two nerve centers of the conquest.

The levying of taxes for the war machine was the first political concern of the conquerors.

The system made a subtle distinction between contributions and taxes. Muslims, though exempt from the latter, were subject to the former, which represented the compulsory 'legal alms', amouting to one tenth of the value of one's immovable property. In addition to a similar tax, the infidels had to pay a personal tax which secured for them the protection of Islam and the right to hold on to their property.

Early in the caliphate, non-real estate revenues fell outside the tax system, which disdained income from such humdrum things as crops and business. Very soon, however, because of the pressing need to come by the new funds required to organize their immense territories, the Omayyads began to tax all gains, and even all merchandise entering a given province, in order to generate local revenue for the governors. This veritable manna was the origin of the embellishment and the blossoming prosperity of the great cities of the Empire.

Justice

However, despite these highly imaginative efforts by the Muslim taxman, the fiscal pressures of Islam were never comparable to ours or to those of the great kingdoms of antiquity.

Another essential figure of Muslim society was the *cadi,* or judge.

This official, whose authority also derived from the central caliphate, was at the governor's side in the administration of justice in towns and provinces.

To begin with, those who held this office were wise and pious, and unanimously respected for their integrity. They handed down rulings full of sound judgment, fair and impartial, trying to follow the moral teaching of the Koran and to present an unblemished picture of an Islam in which justice was equal for all. They were kindly traditional figures in the Arab tales.

Later on the cadi was merely a magistrate sitting in a tribunal and applying a code:

his post having gained in juridical technique but lost greatly in human and political influence.

In Islam justice has always had an aspect of primitive crudity and aggressive equity which was both provocative and exemplary at the same time. Its barbaric corporal element was deliberately shocking: justice was meant to be clear, summary and symbolic, an expression of the divine punishment.

This notion of public degradation and disgrace in the eyes of society is basic to the Muslim approach to the application of the sentence: the convicted person, being guilty in the eyes of God, was stigmatized by his clan of which he was thus unworthy and which, pointing the finger of scorn, rejected him.

The Law of Retaliation, the famous rule of 'an eye for an eye', is the most striking illustration of the Mohammedan conception of a physically implacable form of justice, truly a legal vendetta of society, based on a terrifying parity of damages which bears the stamp more of tribal revenge than of social justice.

It was on the basis of this same principle that unfaithful women were once stoned and that the hands of thieves are to this day chopped off in public in Riyadh.

Such an organization presupposed an administrative structure which had been set up gradually. The first officials who acted as intermediaries between conquerors and conquered were converted Byzantines or Iranians; the Bedouin despised to an equal extent the functions of scribes and merchants. They wanted to be nothing other than the impassioned and mystical fighters of the Prophet.

The army

Moreover the army, that marvelous arm of the Muslim faith and instrument of Arab legend, enjoyed the full veneration and solicitude of the caliphs. The military were a means to conquest and prestige: it was by the sword that Islam spread its power. In fact, for centuries Europeans viewed Muslims exclusively as warriors.

There was no compulsory military service, but each Arab felt that it was his duty and an honor to fight under the banner of Mohammed.

Originally the first conquests were carried out by armed bands of Bedouin who were intoxicated by these warlike excursions which so closely resembled their ancestral marauding raids.

But, as the caliphs denied them their traditional booty by requiring them to spare the property of the infidels, they received, in the form of a pension or lump sum, part of the levies paid by the non-Muslims for their "protection".

This made it necessary at an early date to record the numbers of the troops and to

establish lists of those exempt from service. In other words, the unruly bands of marauders had to be contained within a more conventional military structure. This was particularly important as it no longer sufficed to send out spectacular devastating raids: the conquered territories had to be occupied, and their artistic, commercial and economic potential preserved.

Yet the conquerors' essential weapons continued to be mobility, surprise and enthusiasm: the horsemen of the desert would unfurl in great endless, disorderly waves, sweeping away states just as they had once routed the camps of rival tribes.

As conquest became increasingly difficult and remote, it was necessary to raise ever larger bodies of men, adopt new tactics and create new types of fighting units.

The cavalry, however, remained the elite and the favored arm of the Arab forces, the highest expression of the military life. It alone made it possible to add to one's overall strategy the element of personal daring and spectacular feats of arms. It was also the most effective way of dealing with adversaries who for the most part were slow, static and fearful, paralyzed by these unforeseeable tidal waves of warriors.

The Arab soldier carries within him, as a legacy from the distant past, an uncanny knack for using the slightest irregularity in the terrain to hide and make totally unexpected appearances, spreading panic and terror in the enemy ranks. This "Indian-style" strategy always brought the Arabs their most spectacular successes because it was a part of their inner nature. If one considers for a moment the liberating raids launched by Faisal's Bedouin against the Turks under the leadership of Lawrence of Arabia, it becomes evident that they were merely following the traditions of the Islamic conquerors centuries before.

Such soldiers had obviously to be lightly armed: lance, saber, scimitar, lasso and dagger made up virtually the entire baggage of these whirlwind warriors.

Sometimes, however, the need for sieges and set battles made it necessary to equip certain units with heavier armaments: javelin, club, crossbow (invented in Asia in the 8th century) and the coat of mail (worn by Arab soldiers two centuries before the European armies and always lighter and more flexible than its European counterpart).

They even invented siege machines derived from Roman technology and, as early as the 2nd century, made widespread use of artillery. Their advanced command of chemistry made them the first to use gunpowder; besides the conventional cannonballs their projectiles also included incendiary bombs and vitriol devices.

However, as the Arab temperament was ill suited to this kind of warfare, the manpower for these heavy units was drawn mostly from the populations of the conquered and converted territories or even from legions of slaves.

The army thus gradually acquired a structure and became a powerful machine whose leaders wielded immense influence in domestic decision-making and also in matters pertaining to conquest.

The chiefs, who sat in councils and

appointed the caliphs, had a tight grip on the caliphate, invariably choosing the candidate who could most easily be manipulated. In fact it was they who accelerated the collapse of central power and promoted the separatist tendencies of the far-off provinces. Occasionally they even conspired with provincial governors to set up dissident authority and collect the local taxes for themselves.

If one adds to all this the formation of small private and parallel armies, made up of mercenaries hired by the heads of the most powerful families, it becomes clear that the Empire fell apart as a result of the efforts of those who had actually created it.

There was, however, one area in which the army and its chiefs were above reproach: the faith, which was always intimately linked or merged with the life and function of each individual Muslim.

The essential idea of Muslim society was the close bond between Islam and the state, Islam and the army and Islam and man.

Even so, at the periphery of that society which was primitive and instinctive to begin with and then later on increasingly complex and sophisticated, besides the radiant soldiers, the pampered officials, the exploited converts, the "protected ones" who were both tolerated and under pressure, and the anonymous mass of the people busy in their gardens or their stalls, there was also the crowd of slaves.

The slaves

These too were a part of the Muslim world, just as they had been part of the Christian world.

The notion of egalitarian humaneness expressed in the Koran did not go so far as to condemn slavery, which was solidly rooted in tradition and served everyone's purpose quite nicely. Instead, it merely humanized the institution.

Slaves had to be well treated, well fed and well treated. Yet they had few rights and no responsibility and could hold no political, administrative or religious post. It was recommended that they be emancipated, but with moderation, as they were a necessity: even the poor had their slaves!

A female slave had to serve as a concubine for her master, and was indeed bought for that purpose more often than not. If she produced a son he would be a free man and she herself would become automatically emancipated on her master's death.

If a slave was punished, it was his master who paid; but if the slave suffered some harm reparation was paid to the master.

Gradually, through legal and voluntary emancipations slaves came to be increasingly rare, particularly as it was not possible to replenish their number legally except by taking prisoners of war or committing acts of piracy.

They had therefore to be bought. Since a Muslim could not decently be a slave dealer, the activity itself being outlawed in Islam, it was necessary to go and buy them in Asia, Africa or the Slav countries, from Jewish merchants who dealt almost exclusively in slaves.

No stigma attached to this type of business, which was in fact regarded as essential.

There were certain activities which could be performed only by slaves: dancers, both male and female, singers actors and eunuchs had to be slaves. This status did not rule out sympathy and trust: it was common to leave slaves in charge of one's children, harem or house.

The purchase price depended, of course, on their quality or their special skills. In the 10th century, for example, an adult Abyssinian intended for domestic chores was worth twenty dinars; a black with a more robust build, thirty; a black woman who could act as a concubine, three hundred; a white woman, beautiful and Slav, fetched as much as a thousand!

Diversity and contending factions

When its Prophet died, Islam, though still in its infancy, was about to conquer the world. It was still only a confused stirring of scattered tribes trembling with enthusiasm and faith.

A century later it was one of the most fabulous empires in human history — one which had learnt order, forged its own institutions and devised original and coherent solutions to the problems posed

by its exceptionally vast territorial extent.

It is precisely diversity that is characteristic of Islamic society — its contending factions and even its contradictions which were deliberately maintained out of respect for the personality of the people of each province.

It is quite remarkable that this crazed individualism, far from creating a sterile fragmentation, produced a fantastic explosion of civilization and the development of a culture and a religion which illuminated the European Middle Ages. It was doubtless because Islam, with its content of radiant mysticism, was exactly the kind of demanding but exalting and liberating faith needed by the Bedouin of the desert if they were to move from the patriarchal tribe to the level of a fascinating civilization. In modern times Islamic societies, though having an external structure in the Western style, are still imbued with these contradictory and atavistic principles: an intense individualism impeding any unity and any lasting political harmony; an intact mystical and nationalistic enthusiasm ready to break out in outbursts even after long periods of apparent slumber.

Everything occurs as if the ancient problem of the coexistence of the state and of immaterial Islam had never been resolved since the days of the caliphate.

2. THE MUSLIM FAMILY

The family, which had had a very precise structure since before the time of Mohammed, was the basic cell of Bedouin society.

Through the arrangement of alliances it was the family which gave birth to the tribe and clan. The family was not only a microsociety but also an autonomous economic entity, based on the notion of absolute patriarchy. This omnipotence of the male was something new in the Middle East, where, during the neolithic period the prevailing cult had been that of woman the procreator, the guardian of the home and the person responsible for the domestic pottery, which she fashioned with her own hands long before the advent of professional potterers.

In Islam all this changed: the father was the essential figure whose example was invoked and who acted as the depositary of authority which he then handed down to his male descendants.

However, the intangible rule of custom in early Arab society assured his elder brother, the uncle of his children, an important place in the hierarchy, since it was he who became the new head of the family if the father died.

The status of women

Women, on the other hand, whether wives or sisters depended on the work they did in the family group for the esteem in which they were held. Particularly in rural areas, where their status was even more precarious than in the towns. Yet a wife was one the Bedouin's most valued possessions; indeed he paid in order to be able to marry her, as she looked after his tent and worked like a beast of burden.

She owed total obedience to the husband, with whom, when young, she shared some moments of pleasure before becoming his servant until the end of her days as soon as the hardships of Bedouin life had caused her beauty to fade—which happened very quickly.

While she still had her good looks, however, she was a prey, an object of desire; yet as soon as her charms faded she put on the clothes of a servant and did the servant's work. Her lord and master could whip her, repudiate her and impose on her the concubines of his choice, and even other wives. Fortunately he needed her to ensure the continuity of the male line, the sole glory of the Bedouin, who were above all proud of their race.

It was in this area that Bedouin woman was indispensable; she was accepted at first as a necessary evil and then respected as the mother of the sons of the family.

If she could be the daughter of the paternal uncle this was considered as the ideal arrangement, as the union consolidated the family circle rather than weakening it.

Muslim women had a curious destiny: to be successively sought after for their charms, despised for their impurity and venerated for their fertility.

Mohammed did try to upgrade this equivocal image of the wife, by promising the paradise of Allah to women who satisfied their husbands, looked after the house correctly and gave them sons.

He even tried to improve their social status by giving them legal equality with men and giving them access to inheritances and legal proceedings.

Repudiation, however, continued to the symbol of the arbitrary power of the male. Indeed, the Prophet himself did not hesitate to repudiate two of his wives.

Sterility was usually the reason for this dismissal: first of all because there was no point in keeping a woman who was incapable of producing offspring which could continue the line. The fact of sterility itself was suspect; such a woman was thought to be under some divine curse and could not, for that reason, be allowed to stay under a man's tent.

As for polygamy, which has been so widely misunderstood in the West, there

Above: the delivery of a baby. Right: two Tunisian women wearing the traditional veil.

were several reasons for it: mainly it was intended to increase the chances of an abundance of male offspring; secondly, it was seen as a way of avoiding extra-marital temptations and making it possible to punish adulterous husbands, as advocated, with revolutionary audacity, by the Koran.

Official concubines and legal wives alike were really intended to satisfy the full sensuality of the master within the family cell and to put it to the maximum use to improve the demographic quality of the clan. The Empire badly needed male children to consolidate its conquests and avoid being absorbed by them.

In actual fact, polygamy was more successive and spread out over time than simultaneous. Largely for financial reasons only the rich could afford to support at the same time the four legal wives which the Koran allowed—without mentioning the concubines (often slaves) whose number depended on the whim, or the sexual vigor,

of the master himself. A concubine who was the mother of a son enjoyed the same respect as a legitimate wife; if she was a slave she instantly became emancipated.

This possibility of legally having several wives and concubines provided that they lived in the master's house was supposed to make it possible to do away with prostitution, which was theoretically prohibited by religion.

Actually it was tolerated as a source of revenue, since brothels paid enormous taxes to the state.

Grouped together in the narrow winding streets of the bazaars, the 'houses of ill repute', which were more or less luxurious and richly furnished, accomodated women who lived as veritable recluses. They were not even allowed to go out into the street; in fact the cobblers were not entitled to sell them shoes, so as to make sure that they did not violate the ban!

Children, and especially male children,

were the main thing: Islam badly needed them in order to sustain the explosive spread of its faith throughout the world.

The birth of a child was therefore an occasion for the greatest joy in a Muslim household.

Children

In the words of an old proverb, "Three things gladden the heart of an Arab: having a boy, listening to a poet and seeing the birth of a thoroughbred colt".

However poor he might be, a father was required to display his joy by arranging costly festivities, often resulting in immense hardship.

The birth of the eldest male child gave rise to the greatest merrymaking. Yet each time a male child was born, be he the tenth in the family, the event was celebrated by the entire clan. The arrival of a child in a family was regarded as the blessing of God, the sign that Allah had sought to honor and distinguish the household.

Here again we find the mixture of paganism and religion in the symbolic ritual which marked the coming into the world of the young Muslim.

The offerings intended for the newborn child were allegorical: sugar so that he should be gentle and good; bread so that he should live to a ripe old age; gold so that he should be rich. He was carefully wrapped up so that he would be protected against the evil deeds of the djinns, those malevolent figures of popular mythology which lived in the minds of the ordinary people, together with Allah.

Then he was solemnly baptized and given the name of one of the saints of Islam, at a ceremony attended solely by the family and having no religious character whatever. Thereafter the child would be known by that name attached to his father's name preceded by the prefix *Ben* or *Ibn,* meaning 'son of'. In this way his almost dynastic affiliation and his membership in the venerated family was duly recorded and proudly proclaimed.

He was often better known by the geographical nickname attached to those names, specifying his origins or characteristics. For example, 'Mohammed Ibn Jaffar, al Cordes' means 'Mohammed, son of Jaffar, the Cordovan'. 'Hafez', on the other hand, meant 'who knows the Koran by heart'.

The child was then very carefully raised; whether boy or girl it grew up in the company of its mother in the females' quarters, the famous *harem* from which outsiders were excluded and which, in rich homes, were guarded by eunuch slaves.

If the father died, the custody of the children passed to the paternal uncle.

From the age of five, however, because of that inevitable separation of the sexes which is still so common today in eastern countries, the young persons' lives diverged inexorably. The boy would make his entry into Muslim life with a ritual circumcision— an entirely pagan family ritual which had nothing religious about it.

Adolescents

It is wrong to see in this ritual the equivalent of the Christian baptism. Circumcision, *khitan,* is not even mentioned in the Koran; it is only recommended for hygienic reasons in a region in which water was in short supply, and eventually became part of general custom, to the point where it seemed to be one of the commandments of Islam. It also acquired the status of a rite of initiation and purification, perhaps a reminder of its African origins.

The subject of the operation, feeling none too sure of himself, was led through the village to the accompaniment of a band of heavy drums and shrill flutes.

The procession, consisting of the family and the friends of the clan, headed by the sacrificial barber, gave all due publicity to this happy event.

Having been considered a minor until his initiation, living amongst women and

Even long before Islam rich women used to hide their faces behind veils or leather masks for protection against the rigors of the climate and the desert sandstorms; such coverings were also intended, in some cases, to conceal the ravages of leprosy, which was still common in Central Asia.

Mohammed made the wearing of the veil a symbolic religious obligation, requiring women to show humility and modesty, restraining the ardent passsions of the male and reducing temptation by hiding the female shape and a reminder of the original impurity of woman.

Thus closeted in her sexual segregation the young Muslim girl, before leaving her father's home, busied herself exclusively with domestic and religious concerns, learning to manage the household and venerate Allah at the same time.

But all children, boys and girls, were required to abide by the authority of the head of the family with the most extreme rigor, and respect the traditional rites and taboos: the son could not smoke in the presence of his father, and the daughter was not even allowed to ask him questions.

Their destiny was, of course, set by the head of the family, who had unrestricted control over them, and acted in what he regarded as their best interests and, above all, in keeping with custom.

Schools

At the age of six the boys were sent to the Koranic school; as we shall see, knowledge has always been very important in Islam.

Roughly equivalent to our primary or kindergarten schools, these establishments were situated near the mosque, in the traditional bazaar quarter. Under the strict and implacable discipline of a master who was invariably old and married—symbols of wisdom—they spelt out, entoned and then sang in a chorus their religion and their daily lives.

This way of using the sacred texts to teach reading and grammar to children is one of

protected by the entire clan, the circumcised child now became an adolescent.

He left the cosy tranquility of the harem and thenceforth followed his father, who took charge of his education as a man, taking him into the privileged world of the men in the family.

Young girls, on the other hand, buried themselves ever more deeply in the closed universe of the women. Still free and unveiled at this age, she was destined, at the age of puberty, to become a furtive shadow hidden beneath a dark *chador,* or masked by a veil, the inevitable corollary of the female state.

Right: typical view of a souk. Following pages: the bazaar of Ankara in the 18th century; a council of notables meeting under an oak tree (19th century); inside a nomads' tent; a hanging (17th century); Muslim women in the countryside, and performing a traditional dance at a wedding; two pairs of lovers, the second of them engaged in the consummation of their marriage (16th century); a rejected and desperate lover (16th-century miniature).

countless examples of the deliberate and permanent confusion between religion and daily life. Through the most ordinary acts, Muslim life became an uninterrupted act of faith, impregnating the heart and mind of all concerned.

The most modest school was under the sign of Allah, the supreme master, dispenser of all knowledge and all thought.

Having been thus guided and educated, the Muslim child soon reached the age of matrimony.

Marriage

This event occurred quite early in the Muslim life—nine to ten for girls, fifteen to sixteen for boys—and was the most important act in the believer's life, as Mohammed had proclaimed it to be pleasing to God, whereas celibacy was regarded as a sin and an anomaly.

In the Orient the young man did not make his proposal directly. First he would have the women in his family find out about eligible girls in allied families. This 'espionage' enabled him to focus his choice on an heiress agreeable to his father and whose characteristics seemed in keeping with his tastes—though he himself obviously did not know the girl.

Once the choice had been made and accepted the father would go and make the official request on behalf of his son. He discussed with the prospective bride's father the terms of the contract and the dowry to be provided by the husband.

Fathers traditionally decided on unions between families without consulting the young people themselves, particularly the girl.

When the contract had been signed and the dowry paid, the ceremony could take place with all due pomp. Muslim marriage was a civil and social commitment, and in no sense a religious sacrament. If Allah was present in men's hearts and their prayers, it was purely a personal matter: the Islamic religious hierarchy had nothing to do with this family affair.

The general joy of the family was demonstrated by means of a huge banquet, light displays, crackers, dancing till dawn. The whole village, or at least the quarter, usually took part in the festivities.

Then, escorted by friends and relatives, preceded by musicians, the husband on horseback led the procession followed by the bride who was carried on a litter and whole cartloads of gifts. The nature of the gifts, the relative splendor of the costumes, the number and quality of the musicians were evidence of the social level of the families which were thus being united. It was, after all, an alliance between families, quite as much as a marriage of individuals.

When they reached the bridegroom's house, the spouses entered alone. Only then could the young man raise the veil and contemplate his wife's face. Custom authorized him to repudiate her, before their union was consummated; in such cases, however, the dowry which had been paid remained in the hands of the bride—a fact which made such changes of decision unusual.

The crowd of relatives and friends dispersed only after a bloodstained loincloth had been displayed, as proof of the virility of the husband and the virginity of the bride. Here again we have a rite intended to satisfy the very sensitive honor of the two families.

The taboo of virginity was absolutely imperative when marriage was involved.

The dowry payable by the husband went to the bride herself, as the price of that virginity. In certain regions it was given the appropriate title of 'the Key', or 'the right to the morning', and was viewed as compensation for the loss of maidenhood.

In the past—and even today in some remote Arabian provinces—the bride's father stood at the door to the nuptial chamber rifle in hand, as evidence of his readiness to kill her if she was dishonored.

Left: Bedouin women and children. Below: view of a street at Kairouan (Tunisia).

In such cases the husband was theoretically supposed to expel her immediately.

Divorce

However, once the marriage had been consummated it could be dissolved only through repudiation, generally motivated by the sterility of the bride, or by grave misconduct on her part.

Custom required that the husband, before setting out on a journey or a pilgrimage, should entrust his wife and children to a relative or a reliable friend. He thus provided protection for his family, and at the same time suppressed any temptation that gossipmongers might have had to do him the terrible harm of slandering his family name.

The possibility of divorce existed as early as the pre-Islamic period. Out of deference to custom, Mohammed, though with reluctance, allowed divorce, but he advised strongly against it and attached all sorts of highly deterrent conditions to it, including the loss of the dowry.

Repudiation became definitive only after the completion of the period of the *Idda,* or three menstrual cycles—a safeguard clause, preventing the expulsion of a pregnant wife.

When a couple separated, the children remained the property of the father and were raised by the new wife.

The Mohammed itself is a perfect reflection of these family traditions based on customary law.

Orphaned in the early years of his life, the Prophet was raised by his paternal uncle, to whom he was totally dedicated.

As he grew up with Ali, his cousin, family bonds were definitely involved in the affectionate and indestructible attachment they felt for each other.

The Prophet had a succession of fifteen legitimate wives and as many concubines. At one point he had as many as nine women. Some of them were only seven at the time of marriage, and they had to be left in the custody of their parents for several years before their union could be consummated.

He repudiated three of them—two in circumstances which say much about his character. The first, who was very beautiful and very young, was repudiated because she dared to say to him: "I was given to you against my will and I was not consulted". The second, because she asked him, on the death of Ibrahim, his beloved only son: "How can you be the Prophet of God, if he allows the death of the one being you cherish most in the whole world?"

He was the first to have women veiled in public, and set an example of great family piety, venerating his old mother and Aisha, his favorite wife.

He had only two children: a daughter, Fatima, the wife of Ali; and a son he was immensely fond of, Ibrahim, his sole male descendant, whose death at the age of six put an end to the Prophet's dreams of founding a dynasty. Paradoxically, it was Fatima who, departing from the customary reserved life imposed on women, did most for the posthumous glory of his name.

Funerals

There remained one last stage in the life of a Muslim, before he was presented in the Paradise of Allah: his funeral. This event was quite as public and family-based as the other main rites in his lifetime.

But, just as birth, circumcision or marriage had been joyous, colorful and exuberant, so burial was sober and austere.

Here again, religion played no part; funeral rites were no more of a sacrament than marriage had been. Death was simply the presentation, in a sober and simple manner, of the deceased before God—a personal, private affair.

The body was washed carefully, wrapped in a white sheet and laid out for a last farewell, its face turned towards Mecca.

It was then carried on the shoulders of friends in a procession to the necropolis. All along the way female mourners lamented, singing the virtues of the deceased, tearing their clothes and pulling out their hair with shrill cries, in keeping with a pre-Islamic rite found in many parts of the Mediterranean basin.

Custom required that the procession should be headed by beggars chanting verses from the Koran.

On arrival at the cemetery, where the tomb was already prepared, the body was buried directly on the soil. With its face turned towards Mecca, as a final act of allegiance to the object of the Muslim's mystical faith and an expression of hope for the life to come, the body was laid to rest under a mound of earth.

A simple stone was placed over the graves of the poor, while those of the rich were covered with an elegant brick cupola with four pillars.

Occasionally one might find a sober engraved inscription recalling the deceased's faith—but nothing more. He would then lie there eternally, in the peace of his God, disturbed only on festive days by visits from family or relatives who might come to bring flowers or even eat a meal over the tomb; this latter custom, which dates back to ancient times in the orient, symbolized the permanence of his presence in the hearts and lives of those dearest to him.

Nowadays...

Despite the modern degree of emancipation and the various kinds of 'progress' which have westernized the countries of Islam, the hierarchic relationships within families have not basically changed.

The effect of centuries of ingrained and voluntary habit is so pervasive that these changes can be no more than superficial.

3. HOME AND DAILY LIFE

The Bedouin tent

The first home of the Muslim family was usually one of those elegant, dark tents, characteristically huge and low, which can still be seen along the ancestral routes leading to the seasonal pastures.

They were made of broad strips of black or brown fabric, of goat or camel hair, woven by the women of the family and sewn together to make up the desired surface area.

Held in place by solid wooden stakes, their lower panels could also either be raised to bring relief from the torrid summer heat or padded so as to provide better resistance to sandstorms.

It was in order to survive these devastating storms that Bedouin tents were made flat, almost aerodynamic in shape, and solidly anchored to the ground where they remained, tenacious and robust.

This is the most perfect picture of the typical family cell, with the structure of a micro-society. The interior was entirely covered with carpets and cushions, the only furnishing and indeed the only luxury in the clan. A corner was set aside for women and children, and the rest belonged to the men; the patriarch surveyed the scene royally from a mound of hassocks, respected, if not feared, by all.

All of this exists today, unchanged for many centuries, with the same mint tea offered by way of welcome, and the same piece of saffron-soaked lamb hanging from a stake, in the midst of swarms of flies.

With few minor variations, the nomadic Bedouin of today, of the Maghreb, the Middle East and Central Asia, still live in the closed world of their age-old traditions.

But settled villages, and towns, both big and small, are becoming increasingly common.

The house

The village house was hardly more comfortable or more solid than the tent which it replaced. Molded in blocks of mud mixed with straw, or, in the best of circumstances, built of clay bricks baked in the sun in the old Mesopotamian tradition, it had a flat terrace roof made of dried mud strengthened with palm fronds.

For thousands of years they had all been on one floor: a single entrance, a long corridor and an outer courtyard off which there were a few small dark rooms. Because of the heat there were virtually no external openings; the courtyard provided the family with both air and light.

A thick solid door and a few windows closed with the astonishing wooden grill known as the *moucharabieh,* through which one could observe the life of the street without being seen, served to heighten the sense of reclusion, of isolation of the family in its cool quarters—which, in the Islamic world, was synonymous with comfort and security.

Only the rich had houses with more than one floor—particularly in Yemen—or with a gallery or wooden balcony. Sometimes, in the torrid summer heat of the south, the roofs bristled with tall vents, curious periscope-like objects designed to catch the slightest breath of wind and steer it towards the interior of the dwelling, which was often entirely under ground.

In extreme cases, in southern Iran for example, certain villages had houses dug into the cliffside, with only their façade actually being built, so as to take advantage of the coolness of the earth, not unlike the underground houses built by the Romans in North Africa.

None of them, however, had any water supply to hand, no well and no cistern; water was a collective problem, for the

Left: Bedouin tent. Bottom: typical construction of a ksar in Tunisia.

village or the quarter.

There were also no chimneys or fire-places, doubtless on account of the climate; portable copper braziers sufficed to heat the tent or the house.

Everywhere one went there were carpets and mats, but very little furniture. A bench with cushions—the famous *divan*—was used to seat guests. The most one would find in such dwellings was a few leather hassocks and low damascene tables.

The same sobriety recurred in the domestic utensils: trays made of copper, pitchers, pots, basins and vases, together with some wooden chests for linen and jewelry: such was the extent of the furnishings. On the walls of the houses of the rich there was ornate stucco, mosaics or naive paintings, all evidence of a distinct quest for refinement. In the houses of the poor, the few knick-knacks and mirrors which made up the bulk of the decor were placed in simple niches in the wall.

Hamlets and villages

These houses were clustered together in hamlets or villages, usually fortified in early times on account of the permanent danger of marauding raids—a danger which continued up to the last century.

The entrance was a recessed postern leading to another world, secret and fascinating: the world of long narrow vaulted streets, winding their way past endless blank outer walls of houses; the world of dark porches where a heavy door might swing slightly open as your progress was watched from the shadows; the world of children escorting any strangers that appear in the street and of chickens pecking about their feet; the world of mud-block domes and of pisé ruins scarred by the desert winds; a world of shadows and silence, sheltering the confused to-and-fro of a lethargic life, protected from the rays of the sun which beat down on the tops of walls and terraces.

Miniatures from the 16th and 15th centuries showing architects at work and the construction of a building. Right: oil lamp (19th century). Following pages: in virtually all parts of the Islamic world and at all times in its history, water has been the major concern of Muslims. Wherever it occurs in the middle of the desert a lush palm grove comes into being; in its midst noble architecture was erected. Here we see channels artfully arranged in a garden.

These ephemeral dwellings, being designed for a short life, inevitably disintegrated after a while. In Islam, as in the ancient world, the dwelling of man was temporary: only religious or public buildings were meant to last for ever.

The resulting impression is that of the abandoned vacant lot which is characteristic of oriental towns: as soon as a house collapsed it was left to its fate, and another was built next to it.

Being born of the earth of which it was kneaded by its builders, it gradually returned to that same earth, helping create that feeling of chronic dilapidation which Western visitors find so surprising.

There were numerous mosques, caravanserais, and madrasahs (theological schools) in the towns. The streets, pitted with holes and often littered with filth or dead animals, hardly suggested the presence of so many treasures hidden behind the ochre façades of the houses of rich merchants, opening onto a garden-courtyard embalmed with roses, a blissful refuge of freshness, silence and peace.

The streets were so cramped that it was difficult to see the buildings in their true perspective: travelers had to go up to the terraces in order to get a view of the skyscape, bristling with minarets and gently rounded by the curves of domes which could not be seen from the street. Each part of the town was isolated at nightfall by a heavy gate.

These details clearly illustrate the basic difference between the development of Western towns and that of traditional Arab towns.

In the West each element of the town (houses, monuments) stands out in relief, being built frequently in isolation from clear ground—that is, from a truly urban level! The buildings in any given street can all be seen from the street.

The contrary is true of the Islamic urban structure: here it is the very fabric of the

town that occupies the ground, including houses, the lower part of buildings which are lost in the midst of the whole scene, the bazaars which were often covered galleries and even large numbers of streets covered with vaulting or arcades.

In this way one moves from one enclosed space to another without transition; it is rare to find an isolated monument. In earlier centuries it was not possible to see the monuments of Islamic towns from the street; if it possible now, it is only as a result of the destruction wrought by time or urban planners.

The urban level is therefore not the ground itself—which is never free—but the level of the rooftops, formed by adjacent terraces.

From there it is possible to see the tops of religious buildings—domes and minarets—

Above: the stalls of a bazaar; the apothecary is situated between the jeweler and the butcher. Right: views of a market and a souk (North Africa).

as well as the 'wells' dug into the homogeneous fabric of the town by gardens, inner courtyards and irrigation canals.

It is therefore the rooftops that provide the most striking picture of the traditional Arab towns.

In each town or village the same basic elements of Muslim life are to be found: mosques, hammams, caravanserais, fonduks, madrasahs. All of them blend into the most characteristic fabric of the Islamic town: the bazaar.

The bazaar

The bazaar is basically a market, as well as a meeting place and, occasionally a setting for intrigue, at the economic, social and even political heart of the Islamic town. It is here that people go to talk, buy and circulate.

Whether it be covered with shoddy disjointed paneling or lofty brick cupolas, its galleries or alleys, deep in a permanent penumbra and an equally permanent furnace, occasionally receive a welcome breath of cool air from the splashing fountains.

Its merchants (who have now replaced the caravan drivers of old), its tattered urchins and its wraith-like women clad in their dark veils still give the place a unique kind of animation.

Even today the caravanserais are still to be seen, though now they have been converted into warehouses; its fonduks (lodging houses for merchants) are now general stores. The element of the unusual is always present: incongruous horsemen next to rasping motorized cycles, shopowners taking a nap in their tiny stalls. Businesses, which are exclusively in male hands, are divided up into minute shops, each selling a particular commodity: babouches, fabrics, spices; carpentry, dyers, tanners; leather goods, jewelry.

All concerned work the same way as their ancestors one thousand years ago, following the same immutable traditions, in an atmosphere of cosmopolitan excitement, replete with assorted smells such as perfumes, along narrow alleys the surface of which is often rutted, with the occasional pool of water.

Inside these houses, as under the tents, family life continues in discret and cosy intimacy. The women stay home virtually all the time, busy with their household chores or peering out into the street through the moucharabies.

Muslim society, as we have seen, was designed for men. The boys run along the narrow streets and the adults go and chat in the coffee house over a tea or a rosewater narguile, between periods of work in the fields or the stall.

Sometimes, while playing checkers or chess they even have a chance to drink *nadidh,* a fermented drink made from grapes and dates. But everyone assembles again at home for meals and rest.

Preparation of a meal in the open air.

Meals and drink

Cooking has always been important in Islamic countries; meals ranging from the caravan drivers' banquet to the humblest family dinner have always been accorded great care and refinement. This, of course, is the province of the women. And it is one in which custom and tradition greatly influence diet and the preparation of the food. There are even culinary treatises dating from the time of the Prophet.

In all social classes, down to the lowest, even in the tents of the nomads, the family gathers around low tables or carpets laden with trays and jugs.

The place-setting as we know it does not exist in Islam. Even today among the nomadic Bedouin and in the villages, people use their fingers when serving themselve from the single dish placed in the center of the guests, abiding by a certain order of precedence and making favorable comments about the quality of the food. At the end of the meal it is customary to hand around pitchers of scented water with which the guests wipe their fingers.

Here again we find the mixture of rustic simplicity and refinement which is so characteristic of Islam.

There were even rules of propriety: one should avoid eating too much garlic or onion so as not to offend the other guests; one should not stain one's clothes, suck one's fingers or pick one's teeth in public.

Diet was naturally conditioned by climate and the local possibilities, which differed greatly from one province to another.

According to the Koran it was forbidden to eat dead animals or those killed in any way except by bleeding, as well as pork and dogmeat; that left only the sheep and the goat from the flocks, which were kept for major festive occasions.

Eating such meat was a rich man's luxury

Detail from a banqueting scene.

in which the poor indulged only on special occasions such as weddings, births and circumcisions. The sacrifice of the sheep is as much a ritual symbol as a culinary pleasure. Sometimes to this could be added one of those dry and lanky birds which strut about the desert and virtually raise themselves, with no human intervention, thanks to Allah, near the villages.

Semolina produced by the small fields of meager cereals growing in the oases was the basis of the traditional couscous, the complete and nourishing meal of the poor. The menu was occasionally enriched with garden vegetables: aubergines, asparagus, chick peas, onions, beans, all of which grew wherever there was water.

Cooking was done in sheep fat— usually rancid because of the heat— as butter was a rare luxury in such hot countries. All dishes are strongly spiced with pepper, green and red peppers and numerous aromatic substances such as cinnamon,

ginger, saffron and cloves, which were known and used before the coming of Islam.

For dessert all that was usually available was the large red water-melons which were so common throughout the Empire; sometimes dates, figs or almonds could be had, depending on the region.

The gardens and orchards of the Arab oases were in fact very productive and very rich; their produce, however, was usually reserved for the rich, while the poor had to content themselves with milk soup, stew, couscous and water-melons.

Even today, although town-dwellers have access to normally stocked markets, their purchases depending on the size of their purse, the nomads or the peasants of the remoter villages are economically constrained to the same ascetic frugality.

The homes of the rich, however, were familiar with caviar, roast poultry or lamb, grey truffles from the Arabian desert, fruit

pastes, *lukums,* flower preserves and delicacies made with honey.

The national drink is water and tea, often scented with green mint. Coffee, which was not introduced until the 14th century, was specially prepared, 'Turkish style', by means of infusion. But it never became as common or as popular as the traditional tea.

As for wine it was known and liked throughout Islam. But because of the prohibitions contained in the Koran, the cultivation of the vine and the manufacture of wine were left to Christians and Jews.

The accursed beverage was thus made by infidels, glorified by poets, and also consumed—as a matter of course by kings, and furtively by the ordinary people.

This wine, which was 15° proof, was not of very good quality.

The heat greatly impeded the making and, in particular, the conservation of wine. Since casks were unknown, the wine was transported and stocked in large green bottles, either flat or balloon-shaped, which were sent as far as India.

Clothing

Rest was also a communal affair: people used to stretch out on mats and carpets, as beds were originally not used as furniture. The sexes were segregated even in the cramped conditions preveiling in the tents, and promiscuity was thus curtailed: separate quarters were provided for women and children, depending on their social rank.

This background of habitual intimacy was punctuated by occasions on which it was necessary to appear in public—to go to the bazaar, the mosque, the shop or the fields.

And for such occasions the correct attire was essential: it could vary according to one's family's wealth, but was in the traditional style. External appearances being very important among orientals, clothes were in themselves a sign of prosperity: the elegance or magnificence of garments worn in public were a way of honoring one's guests.

Though differing in detail from one province of Islam to another, dress was, nonetheless, subject to certain common rules: the peasant of the desert or the caravan-driver went about draped in a long robe of white or beige fabric, protecting his face with a long turban, the *shesh;* a rich merchant would wear roughly the same type of garments, but cut from silk or fine linen and enhanced with more or less brilliant brocade; caliphs, viziers and high state dignitaries wore special 'robes of honor' in the presence of distinguished visitors.

For Muslim women personal appearance and dress have always been a way of making up for the drab humility imposed on them by the seclusion in which they were required to live.

The luxury that all of them dreamed of was to wear clothes made of those fairy-like fabrics woven from gold and silver thread which one still sees in abundance in today's bazaars and souks.

Female coquetishness was also exercised by means of the brightly colored and sprangled Turkish slipper, or babouche; bodices decorated with fine embroidery, and full skirts made of fine fabrics which flashed a thousand colors as one walked along.

Sophistication was possible even in the veil: tulle, Chinese silk, muslin from Mossul and embroideries cut in the form of smaller veils represented the very height of refinement.

Of course all these things were very expensive; accordingly the poorer classes relied mainly on dyes to liven up their dull attire. For that reason, the dyers who worked with skins, wool and fabrics were the most prosperous craftsmen in medieval Islam.

In winter everyone wore long cloaks woven from goat and camel hair or sheep's wool.

Leather from Cordova and Morocco was extensively used, either dyed or in its natural state. It was made into saddles for horses, hassocks and cushions, and ceremonial belts and boots, the female versions of which were fine and ornate.

Segregation occurred even in the traditional Turkish slipper, which was red or brown for the poor, and yellow or black for the rich.

However, with the exception of ceremonial regalia, ordinary day-to-day dress consisted of two main seasonal items having only local or social variants: full, thick and warm cloaks, of which the North

African burnous is a good example; garments of fabric, light in both color and weight, becoming whiter and finer as one mounted the social ladder. Lastly, luxury garments used only by rich families and made with all the refinement made possible by active trade with the Far East. Depending on the province, headgear consisted of sheshias, turbans or agals for the men, veils or chadors for the women, and felt caps for the slaves.

Men of high social rank, clad in black or white silk, went about only on horseback, riding Arabian thoroughbreds. Now they drive about in Mercedes.

The fellahs, when going either to the shops or the fields on the oasis, wore clothes of darker colors, which stained less easily and lasted longer.

Whatever their social class, women found ways of indulging in coquettishness. Besides fine fabrics, jewels and perfumes were the means they used.

Perfumes and jewels

The art of the distillation of flowers had given Islam a profusion of scents which were used by women and even by men.

Essences of rose, jasmine, amber and lemon were stocked in abundance by the tiny shops in the traditional *attarin* souk, reserved for spices and scents, the aroma from which flavored the whole of the oriental market.

Not to mention henna, which was used to dye the hands and hair, and khol for making up the eyes.

In these markets women also bought miraculous powders made from lizards, fetuses, and ground gazelle or mandrake horn which they, in their pagan superstition, viewed as a panacea for their marital problems: indeed, these aphrodisiac remedies were reputed to be the best protection of the unity of married couples.

The jewels which had been invented since the earliest times for the adornment of women were not lacking in the Muslim home. Yet, apart from enhancing female beauty, they also had another meaning in the Islamic orient; they were intended as a religious symbol, though they were in fact quite as pagan as amulets, and they also represented the family's equity, in the form of precious metals and stones.

When the harvest was good, when a camel or sheep was sold, it was customary to buy a bracelet or a necklace. Conversely, when times were bad, women used to sell off their jewelry to raise cash. These transactions were the monopoly of small jewelers, traditionally Jewish, who in each souk or bazaar played the uncertain but socially necessary role of goldsmiths, pawnbrokers and moneylenders.

These jewels were traditionally made of gold or silver. The silver ones, which were more common than their gold counterparts in the homes of the lower classes because of the abundance of that metal in the ancient world, were best adapted to the rural life, being cheaper and more solid while being big and bright enough to impress. Silver was also the symbol of frankness and purity, and thus very much in harmony with the harsh life in the desert. This was the ornamental metal most used by the nomads and the womenfolk of the remote villages.

Gold jewels, which were vastly more expensive, were also smaller, apparently miniatures of those made of silver. They were worn by towndwellers whose high living and frivolity seemed very much in keeping with the corruption and vice which the metal symbolized. Many a local sheikh in the oases on the caravan routes of the desert would not even touch gold with their hands, for fearing of being sullied: instead, they used sticks!

Gilded silver, enamels and filigree, inlaid with multicolored hard stones had also been in use since the earliest times.

Whatever the material, however, the form and symbolism and Muslim jewels

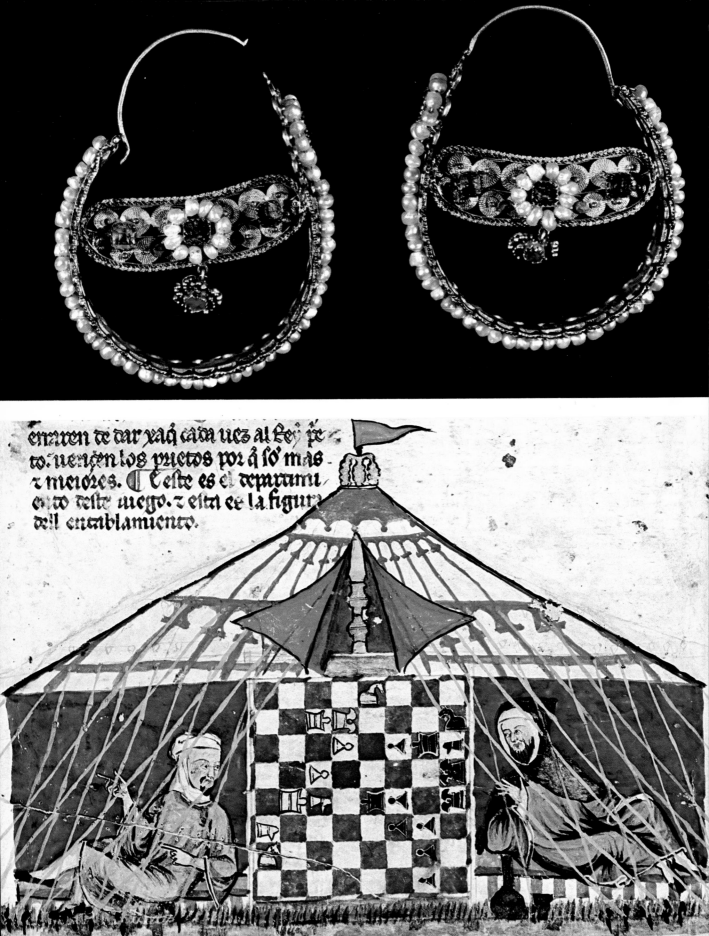

للإذمان وَهِلِ مِفتَةِ الوزن والإدمان وَعَلَمَكَ بالكَب
ني كُلَّ الأوقات

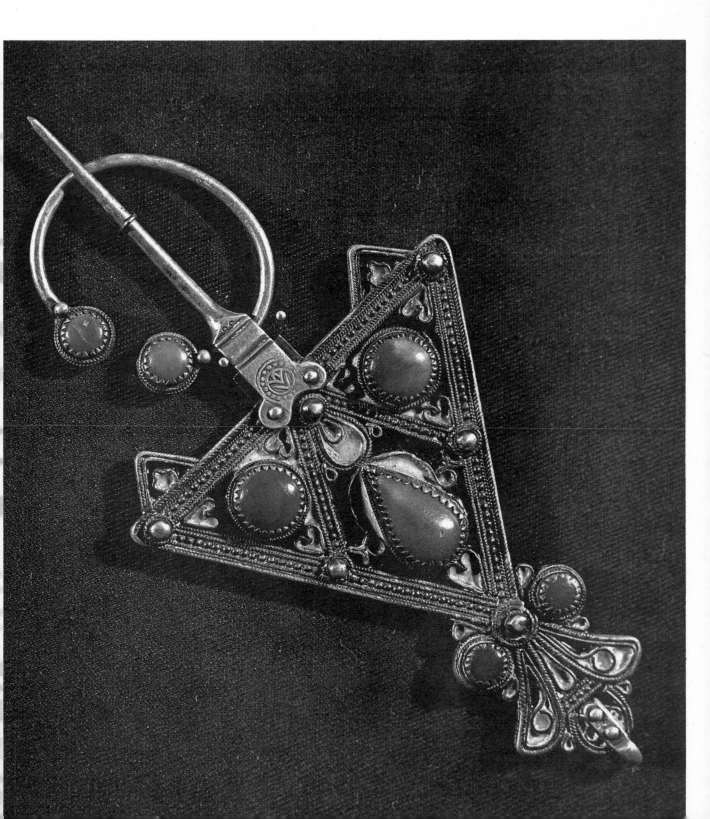

remained immutable.

Although their shapes may have been borrowed from recent Roman antiquity, or the ancient civilizations of the orient (Indus, Syria, Mesopotamia and Egypt), their originality of cut and decorative detail is beyond doubt.

Certain jewels were essentially functional: hairpins, belt buckles, clasps, clearly derived from the Roman *fibula*. Others were purely ornamental: pendants, pectorals, diadems, earrings, necklaces, ankle and wrist bracelets, rings.

Apart from the fact that some of them may be useful for purposes of defense (bracelets and rings), as among the Romans and Sassanids, all of them were really intended to have votive and symbolic significance which, though apparently religious, is actually pagan, superstitious and fetishist. They were really talismans in which one can see the ritual ancestral motifs, either in the central theme of the jewel or the series of amulets which hung from it:

The fish, a Semitic and not particularly Christian sign, providing protection from the evil spirits, as the fish, under the water, was beyond the reach of malign fate;

The hand, the Phenician sign of Baal, regarded as a good-luck token;

The dove, universal symbol of love;

The crescent and the moon, also Phenician attributes of the goddess Tanit, assimilated to Juno, protector of women;

The heart, derived from the *bulla* which young Romans wore about their neck, possibly a stylized form of the lock of the house and home;

Arches, representing the door of the home or the mosque;

'Traces', a highly original graphic form borrowed from the empirical art of the nomads and showing in stylized form the 'traces' left in the sand by the animals of the desert: gazelle, lion, horse, jackal. All of these were seen as a protection against the evil eye.

Lastly, certain jewels had noise-makers attached to them (bells, granular metal) or scents (sandalwood, musk, amber) which were thought to have aphrodisiac powers.

Others which were rarer and even more valuable, took the form of small boxes containing cabalistic papers or beneficent substances. Some of them had verses from the Koran engraved on plaques of agate or metal.

one's pleasure, provided that one was a man. First, the coffee house. Actually this term is not quite accurate, as the place in question consisted of a huge room where men crowded around usually empty tables to take their turn smoking the *narguile,* the famous collective water-pipe, which was passed from hand to hand.

Tobacco, which was imported only as late at the 16th century into Arabia, burned in a cupule over embers kindled by suction. And the smoke had to bubble its way through the perfumed water of a flask before being inhaled, when thoroughly scented and purified, virtually without nicotine.

In such gathering places one went to hear public storytellers reciting the works of the most famous poets or rehashing the eternal stories about the battles and exploits of the warriors of the conquest, the real mythological heroes of Islam. These endless sessions were occasionally punctuated by a round of mint tea.

It was also possible to play chess and drafts, both of which were very popular among the Arabs.

In certain provinces the men used to meet to smoke hashish or chew *qat*, because of the euphoria thus obtained and because both of these substances helped quell the pangs of hunger and, in the most wretched circumstances, instil a feeling of optimism. Such practices were so widely accepted that euphoric 'herbs' innocently found their way into the ingredients of certain sweets, pastries and preserves, mixed with ginger, cinnamon and cloves. This had been done since the most ancient times without the slightest intention of finding an 'artificial paradise' or the slightest feeling of degradation.

The hammam

The Muslim bath, the *hammam,* which was recommended by the Koran, derived directly from the Roman baths. Like them, it was based on the need for hygiene, since

Entertainment

The life of a traditional Muslim home, once the traditional daily business and duties had been discharged, left little room for entertainment, apart from the family feasts which occurred on certain significant occasions of the life of the believer, from the cradle to the grave.

But it should be clearly understood, however, that the merrymaking of a family feast and also prayer itself were a part of the joys of the Muslim, just as a woman derived pleasure from the act of decking herself out in her finery and a warrior knew the excitement of galloping across the desert on a superb thoroughbred stallion.

One could, however, go out to obtain

there was no water in individual houses. And it followed a similar evolution, as this utilitarian function became transformed into a refined form of relaxation which rich and poor enjoyed together. Before Mohammed there had been no public baths in Arabia. It was he who caused such baths to become so popular. From the 10th century there was one per quarter, and they were always well attended. On one day each week they were reserved for women and children.

Since then they have greatly increased in number with each passing century, and they still exist today, in both towns and villages, and are quite as well attended as in the past, despite the progress made in private plumbing.

It should be unterstood that this was no mere bath-cum-shower.

Like their Roman model the Muslim baths consisted of several rooms: a changing room, a cold water room, a hot water room, a sweating room, a massage room and a resting room. All of these had marble walls and mosaic floors, and were arranged around a central vestibule covered by a dome with translucid portholes.

Sports and falconry

The sports which are now so widely developed in the Islamic countries, as elsewhere, are really pastimes which have a much more Indo-European than a Semitic origin. The idealization of effort, the gratuitous cultivation of muscular excellence are concepts which are not particularly characteristic of the Arab world.

However, archery, polo, croquet, fencing and the javelin were practised not just for their military applications but also as sports. But the most popular sports of all were horse racing and camel racing in Arabia, cock and dog fighting in Afghanistan and mock fighting on horseback.

Turkish wrestling, between heavyweight bare-chested giants, wearing leather pants and covered with grease to make themselves harder to grasp, is still very popular.

The same is true of the *Zour Kaneh* of Iran, games combining religion and gymnastics in which men of all social backgrounds—merchants, workmen, bank clerks—meet every evening. They collectively and skilfully manipulate huge wooden clubs or strange panels in the form of shields weighed down with chains, to the mesmerizing rhythm of a drum accompanying chanted verses from the Koran.

Another purely Arab passion is falconry. It was also imported from Sassanid Persia, together with its rites and vocabulary. It survives intact in the Gulf Emirates, where the sheikhs spends small fortunes for the rarest and best trained falcons to go hunting (in their Mercedes) in the desert.

Such is Muslim life. And one should not think that it has changed so very much today.

Left: a snake-charmer, another figure traditionally found at open-air gatherings. Below: reconstruction of a reception room (Mankind Museum London).

4. RESOURCES AND WORK

The economy of the Muslim world was based on trade.

As the geographic situation of the Empire makes of it a link between the worlds of the Mediterranean and those of Central Asia, it was only normal that there should be permanent, intense and active commercial ties between the West and the Far East, passing through the Middle East.

But the Islamic state was not content merely to be an intermediary. Very soon, with the same dynamism and the same intelligence as it displayed in both letters and sciences it developed its own method of trading and devised new types of products which were to make it one of the most powerful economic empires in the world. In a few centuries the driving force of its agriculture, industry and commercial networks achieved spectacular results.

Agriculture

For obvious reasons agriculture was possible only in the oases and those areas which has a privileged climate: the Caspian, Southern Yemen, the Black Sea, the Indus, etc.

Long before Islam, as soon as neolithic man had evolved from a wandering/ gathering type of life to a sedentary mode of production, he devised ways of using even the smallest plot of irrigated land for livestock and a few meager crops. In Arabia this was a particularly difficult and thankless task. Within a feudal and tribal structure strongly reminiscent of the status of the serfs in the Middle Ages in Europe, the fellahs eked a living from the soil, but hardly produced enough for trade.

From the time of Mohammed onwards a humanitarian concern and the need to

Left: a peasant woman in a rural area. Below sharpening a millstone.

Left, top and below: peasants, one of them cutting a plant and the other sifting grain. Bottom left: cattle-driver with his animals.

feed the increasing population of the young state led the first caliphs to take a close look at the fate and the yield of the peasants of Arabia.

Draft animals gradually made their appearance: the dromadary, the horse, and the buffalo from Irak replaced the fellah who used frequently to harness himself to the plow next to his donkey.

For many years the tools used remained primitive and ancestral: iron plowshares did the work better and faster, yet they had a hard time replacing the ritual wooden adze.

It is evident that the farmers of Islam were also familiar with the notion of the enrichment of soil by means of crop rotation and fertilizers, these latter being of course provided naturally by the manure of the animals.

In Iran, Shah Abbas had the original idea of producing on the industrial scale the organic fertilizers needed for the development of farming in the oases by means of the intensive raising of pigeons in huge pitted powers—genuine guano factories.

Yet this development of agricultural production was obtained above all through the efforts of man who still, however, preserved his old superstitions and age-old magic remedies: for example, in order to get rid of the tares which invaded the fields, it was thought to be enough to have a virgin run around the field one night carrying a rooster!

The nomads, who were ill-disposed to sedentary agriculture, preferred to become shepherds and follow their flocks along the eternal seasonal routes. Yet they managed to improve and, in particular, to increase the volume of their stock which, having originally been merely an additional support for the family, eventually became a full-scale commercial operation: black goats in Iran, astrakhans in Central Asia, cattle on the Caspian, horses in Trans-oxania, and sheep and camels everywhere.

But agriculture and livestock both depend, ultimately, on water. While the nomadic shepherd could content himself with tracking down the poor pastures which were sustained by a very occasional shower (a few minutes' rainfall being enough to cause a short-lived pasture to cover the dunes with green), the farmer in such a climate needed permanent running water. For thousands of years, therefore, irrigation has been the key to farming of any sort in the Middle East; gradually it devised its own solutions and techniques, rudimentary but effective.

Sometimes there are wells which suffice for year-round farming. Large leather waterskins pulled by camels shed their precious load into small channels which distribute it throughout the oases, where

it is quickly soaked up by the parched sand.

The Arabs were the inventors of the waterwheel, or *noria,* the huge structures which can still be seen along the roadside, driven by the current of the river and tirelessly irrigating the nearby gardens.

In extreme cases, long before Mohammed, they had the ingenious and curious idea of digging *ghanats,* long underground canals, all excavated by hand, which drained off the slightest drop of moisture in the soil and channelled it into a tiny stream.

In areas where these canals have been dug, the desert seems to be elevated by rows of giant molehills, about 60 to 90 feet apart, formed by vertical wells used in the digging of the *ghanats.*

These capricious lines of pimples of yellow ochre sometimes range as far as 30 to 50 miles into the desert, where they carry water drained from the foot of remote mountains which block the horizon.

The well-diggers of the desert, whose traditional expertise was passed down from father to son, were responsible for keeping these canals permeable: they would stay five or six hours at the bottom of the tunnels in order to dig a mere 12 to

15 feet of main shaft; the earth thus excavated was hoisted to the surface in a small box by means of a wooden winch straddling the opening to the shaft. This accounts for those conical heaps of rubble which help one trace, as far as the eye can see, the mysterious underground route taken by the miraculous water, the sole umbilical cord of this inhuman world.

In other regions the water was stocked in vast underground tanks covered with a cupola of puddle clay to protect the ground water, which could be reached by a flight of stairs and was kept cool by a giant ventilator shaft designed to capture the slightest breath of air.

In all regions bordering on the desert each hamlet had its own—every often only the end of a *ghanat.* They were situated next to tall pointed cones, a kind of termite-mound made of unbaked brick, reminiscent of the lids placed over a plate of couscous.

These were the *yakh-chai* which were used throughout the Middle Ages as a kind of icebox: their very thick walls made it possible, apparently, to keep chunks of ice or layers of snow, which had been brought

down from the mountains and carefully insulated between thick layers of straw, for many months until the hottest part of the summer.

All of these methods made it possible for the maximum number of nomads to live the settled life and for agricultural output to increase.

Very soon, in the privileged regions— Southern Yemen, where the rhythm of crops was based on the monsoons; the Caspian Sea, which had the benefit of Russian rainfall; the Kol Delta, which was fertilized by seasonal floods; and the South of Spain, which was singularly fertile —the efforts of the peasants led to exceptional amounts of produce, with the help of the progress made by agronomic science.

Even so, each harvest was an occasion for popular pagan feasts in which heaven was thanked for its lifegiving generosity.

Accordingly, from the 10th century onwards, there was no idleness in the orchards and gardens of Islam, where work was regulated by the rhythm of the seasons.

Rice, beans, pomegranates and indigo were harvested in September, and the henna was removed; in October, the orange and banana groves were protected; in November, barley, hemp and wheat were planted; in winter, the olives were picked and the poppy was planted in a position sheltered from the wind and the cold. At the end of winter the sugar cane was harvested and cotton was planted; henna was planted in spring.

With the exception of potatoes and tomatoes, all the vegetables and fruits which we have today came from the oases where they had existed since the 9th century. Celery, aubergines, artichokes, cucumbers, and pumpkins were the most popular.

And one should not forget the numerous aromatic substances which the Arabs are so fond of: marjoram, aniseed, mint, basil, saffron, peppers, oregano and fennel.

The orchards spoken of so glowingly by the poets produced almonds, blackberries, carobs, pomegranates, apricots and figs. There were even special horticultural establishments at which attempts were made to grow new plants imported from all parts of Asia.

From the 12th century onwards there were treatises of horticulture which taught ways of fertilizing date palms by shaking the male flowers on the female pistils so as to increase the output of fruit. Other works, even at that early date, described the technique for pruning some fifty or more fruit trees and the vine, and also methods for carrying out grafts and the planting of cuttings.

The same was true of the breeding of silkworms, which were imported from China, and also bees. Oriental silk invaded Western markets during the Middle Ages, and honey was so common that it was used in Persia as a means of paying taxes in kind.

From the 12th century the number of textile plants under cultivation grew considerably: cotton in southern Turkey, Iran and Irak; hemp in the Nile Delta. There was a similar profusion of what might be described as 'industrial plants': madderwort, the roots of which were used to produce red dye; indigo, a proud shrub which produced the dye of the same name; henna, a herb cultivated for the tan tincture extracted from its leaves and used, for many years, as the sole makeup of Bedouin women. Lastly, there was the opium poppy, dispenser of opium and dreams.

Flowers were the most distinctively Arabic crop of all: not just for the greater beauty of poets' gardens, but also for the distillation of essences and perfumes: rose, violet, jasmine, aloe, which were abundant in Arabia and Persia; water lilies from Albania; wild lemons from the desert; balsmodendrons from Yemen which provided an aromatic resin, myrrh; boswellia from Abyssinia and Arabia, which secreted a highly prized aromatic resin, incense.

As can be seen there is a huge gap between the first Bedouin fellahs toiling endlessly over their tiny oasis, generated by a trickle of water from a *ghanat,* and the marvelous gardens of Saadi in the Shiraz of the 10th century, or those of Moorish Andalusia.

What had once been a small crop needed for individual survival had become an opulent and highly organized agriculture which transmitted to the West species from the remote Orient which had hitherto been unknown.

An important bonus of all this agricultural activity was the remarkable art of the Arab garden, a subtle and refined artistic creation, a tribute to the permanent miracle of the water provided by Allah to fertilize the desserts.

Industry

Agriculture was the first, the most elementary and the most universal acquisition of settled man. Industry, on the other hand, made its appearance much later and more locally as it was necessary for raw materials and technology to be available in the same place at the same time. It was therefore only gradually that men living in settlements came to be metallurgists and craftsmen.

At the time of Mohammed, the Middle East, and more particularly Arabia, had made virtually no progress in this field, which remained virtually unchanged from the days of the great civilizations of antiquity.

Metallurgy

It was at first handicapped in Islamic countries, as in the Orient in ancient times, by the absence of coal and the Paucity of supplies of wood, with the consequent difficulty of obtaining fuel. The few seams of coal (on the edge of the Iranian plateau, in Zagros and Anatolia) which had sustained the metal workers of antiquity (Tepe

Yaga, Luristan, Yazelikaya, etc.) were put to use once more, while those in need of fuel proceeded blithely to strip bare the few remaining forest regions in order to smelt metals.

The metals were difficult to use, more often than not, since ores were both relatively inaccessible and of rather poor quality.

Yet the factories which had been opened up in numerous parts of the Islamic world to support the drive for conquests and, later on, the greater volume of trade, worked at maximum capacity with the help of increasing numbers of African slaves.

Ores were transported to sites just outside the towns, where they were smelted for the most part in wood-fired ovens.

Zagros produced gold, silver and mercury; Armenia, borax and antimony; Afghanistan, silver, copper and lead; Cyprus continued to supply copper and Nubia gold, while most of the mountain ranges (Zagros, Anatolia, Beluchistan, etc.) were full of iron ore. Tin alone was rare.

Once smelted in this way, the metals—whether pure or in alloys—were cast and shaped, becoming pitchers, dishes, vases, trays, goblets, chandeliers, braziers, caldrons or weapons.

Just as agriculture created the delicate art of gardens, so metallurgy led to the blossoming of craftsmanship of a very high order: hammered or carved trays; ornamental ironwork flowering forth in a profusion of balustrades, grills or moucharabies of wrought iron; inlaid work with gold or silver thread and ivory or mother-of-pearl marquetry.

All these techniques led to the brilliant outpouring of works of art from Mossul, Damascus, Baghdad and Spain. 'Damascene' work, used to adorn trays, rifle butts and chests, swept across Europe. The region of Bukhara and Samarkand became famous for the sophistication of its remarkable decorative work with bronze.

But there was never an 'industry', in the proper sense of the term; production, which was deliberately limited, continued to be on a craft basis, the work of small stalls and family workshops. Moreover, as a sign of their wisdom, Muslim creative craftsmen never moved beyond the stage of personal work and original production, thus preserving their own style, despite the stereotyped nature of themes and decorative symbolism. When techniques from the Far East were to be transmitted to the Moorish West, there was never a mere copy: ingenuity and subtle refinement always proved able to transform the act of creativity by embodying in it the Islam soul, amalgamated with the personality of the craftsman himself.

Cabinet-making

To some extent because of its rarity, wood was always a highly prized material in the Middle East.

Where wood occurred naturally it was used as a material in that same area: for example, the date palms provided—as they still do—the lumber for the house frames, doors and bridges in the southern oases.

Later on imported woods were used, such as cedar from Lebanon.

In this way balconies, balustrades, loggias and moucharabies were gradually fashioned.

Here again we are dealing with craftsmen and their individual output, and not a commercial-scale enterprise.

Unlike metallurgy, which required large amounts of labor, at least for the extraction and transport of the ores, woodworking was done by individual craftsmen according to their own taste, at their own pace and in response to local demand.

Glass

Glass, which had been invented by the Phenicians, was very widely used in Syria and the Middle East at the time of the Prophet's birth.

As early as the 10th century products

ورا العشرة الثالثة هو اسله وانكاره والسائله هو اصنعت • واما في الده ما كان وجعله اشد
يسيرا وهوزائل عن النفس • • وورا العشرة الخاوية وما ذنه نسيره
وحدثها وكونها ورا العشرة السائله على نفس النقا الحدقه
والسواد بعد اصناف في احدها ان يتوا

أمْرَاضُ القَرِينَة

السبب	العلامة	...	...	...
	الاسقراع النديان الكلى			

القصد

انكار اللون

منقلبا

نوكه

بوص السبح

والسكر

القصدان تباف

حمل العسل

سو هم من راه اند سرو الدقيقه بينهما ان السكون العسد ان سكانت العين الحلا او سهلا اورق
النوسى العنى شبه العنه • والماء اذبعلوا السوحى يصال هذا العسل • والرابع يسى
والساض اذال الباض يعرض عن الله الذى نعمه القرينه

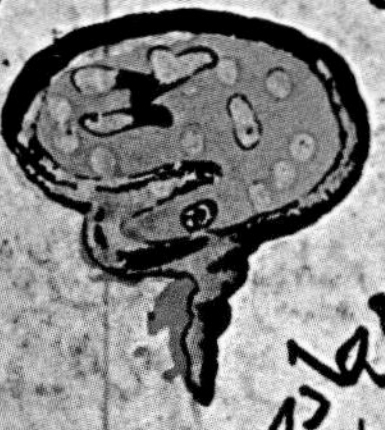

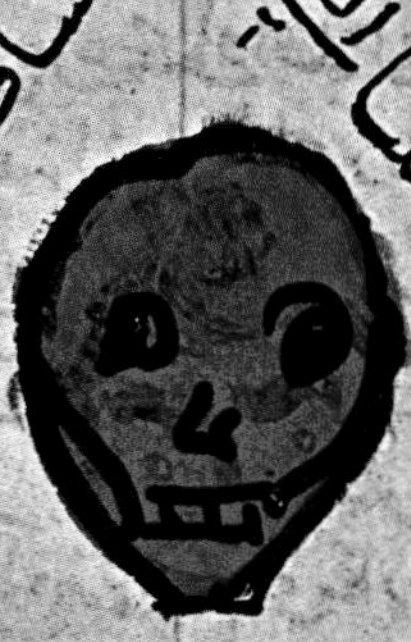

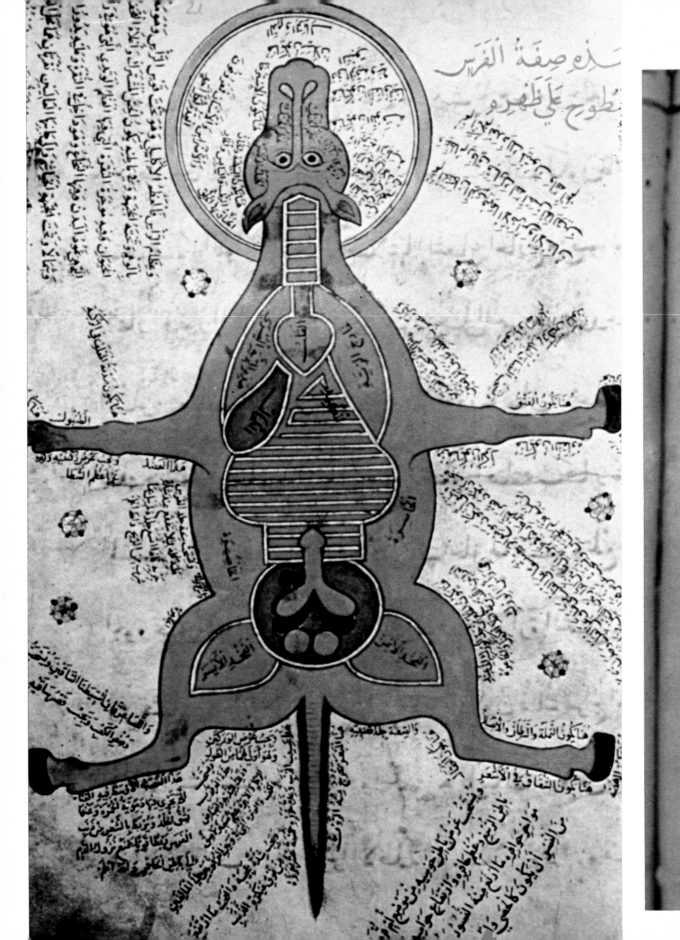

حو الذراع

قطّافها زهرہ قتيـ

هر الكذيرة على ط

القضبان ومنـ

خوشبيةً بهذا

اكبه ورقًا منه و

تفترش على الار

نباته وزهرہ ام

الغزفيريّة وكلا

اذا دقّ احدهـ

ماؤه قتيًا بلغمًا

كان من اجود

البلغمية لذلك وهو ينوّم ويحلّل النفخ وينفع م

وقد يشرب طبيخه لتسكين حرارة الدّم وعصاب

حتى صار صاحب أمه

Left: a mandolin player (painted ceramics, 11th century, Islamic Museum, Cairo). The brightness of the reproduction shown below is due to the fact that it is a painting on glass (Hazem Palace, Damascus).

were already being sold in throw-away glass containers!

Here again the evolution of techniques was very prodigious. Flasks of all sorts; bottles for perfume or wine, the latter being flat for purposes of concealment about the person; retorts and test-tubes for the fledgling science of chemistry. From the 11th century onwards glass window panes were in use—transparent, irridiscent or translucid—but only in the houses of the rich or public buildings.

Glass also managed eventually to free itself from utilitarian constraints and achieve artistic expression, particularly in the form of colored glass paste, sometimes covered with enamel, or irridiscent with metallic reflections. The ultimate achievement of this quest for beauty was the polychrome stained glass in use in the 12th century.

There is no doubt that this artistic technique for working with glass came, from Egypt and Syria, to Europe, where it enabled the Venetian glassmakers of Murano to produce their prodigious works of art between the 13th and 17th centuries.

Paper

Until the time of Islam, and ever since antiquity, records had been inscribed on rolls of papyrus or parchment; books were unknown.

Paper was invented by the Chinese; in 712 Samarkand was the capital of fine

paper, which was obtained from a hemp paste which has been soaked and then stretched in thin sheets and dried.

In 794, however, the first Islamic paper factory opened in Baghdad; it used hemp at first, and then changed to cotton, which was more abundant in the Empire.

This technique, which was soon simplified and thus made less costly and more productive, spread through Spain to medieval Europe.

Binding, which was also imported from China, was similarly disseminated from the 10th century onwards.

By the 13th century, a whole century before Gutenberg, Islamic printers were using special papers and bronze characters dipped in organic inks or tinctures.

Pottery and ceramics

Pottery was the first form of craftsmanship achieved by neolithic man in the Middle East; quite soon it became his most perfect form of artistic expression.

Though originally kneaded by the female custodians of the household, it became, with the invention of the oven, the sphere of specialized craftsmen who found themselves expelled from the towns because of the danger of fire which their installations posed to all around them.

The Arabs and the Islamicized peoples had thus always had utilitarian pottery, such as jars, dishes and domestic objects.

Even though the shapes used were still those inherited from antiquity, they soon added their own personal touch through the introduction of a revolutionary process which involved mastery of the application of colored enamel on terra cotta.

In ancient times polychrome varnished bricks had already been used by the Assyrians and then by the Achemenids to adorn their temples and palaces.

But it was the Arabs of Islam who disseminated this process, by lining their sanctuaries.

The great mosques of Baghdad, Tabriz and Isfahan were soon covered with blue enamelled bricks.

From the 10th century onwards, the town of Kashan, on the central plateau of Iran, became specialized in the manufacture of these polychrome tiles, which were known thereafter as *kashi*. Arabs, Mongols, Timurids and Sefevid Persians then succeeded each other in using them for their religious buildings.

The technique involved spreading over the bricks a coat of lapis-lazuli blue or turquoise green vegetable or mineral tincture (i.e., using the colors of the Prophet and of Islam) and then baking them in ovens where they became vitrified. It was even possible to add irridescence to the enameled polychrome surface by releasing the vapors of oxidized gases during the baking process, thus imparting a moiré finish with a highly prized metallic sheen.

This process was used for formal dinner ware and architectural finishings. For the decoration of large surfaces it was customary either to juxtapose monochrome tiles, producing a pattern by the arrangement of individual tiles, as in mosaics; or by putting in place enormous panels which already contained the motif, completely drawn and enameled.

This presupposed a mastery of the technique of simultaneously baking several tinctures, each of which had a specific point of vitrification, sometimes several hundred degrees apart.

All of these problems had been resolved by the 14th century, and no further evolution took place in the technology for making glossy ceramics.

Thenceforth progress was focussed on the finesse or luxuriance of the motif and the technical virtuosity of the craftsmen laying the tiles—both of which reached their apogee under the Sefevids in the 17th century.

The laying of mosaics of glossy ceramic

This page: Tunisian woman decorticating plants, for use in the dyeing of fabrics depicted in the manuscript page shown below. Right: weaving in a Jordanian village.

tiles is actually a fantastically difficult task: the execution, petal by petal, of a single enamel flower took more than a whole day of effort from a workman so expert that he truly qualified as an artist. This gives one an idea of the sheer number of craftsmen involved and of *kashis* used: it took more than a million and a half of varnished tiles 10 inches square to line the great royal mosque of Isfahan!

The chemical industry

Chemistry and alchemy were merged together in medieval minds; for the Arabs all metals were variants of the basic metals, gold and silver. All one had to do, therefore, it seemed, was to find favorable physico-chemical conditions to transform iron or copper into gold!

This dream of the 'philosopher's stone', shared by all alchemists of the Middle Ages, was very common in Islam from the 10th century, when scholars were trying to discover the mysterious substance, or *al-iksir,* which would make it possible to change the lowest minerals into precious metals.

On the way, however, they discovered and perfected processes to obtain the tinctures which were abundant and widespread in the Western world. For example, indigo blue, from the flowers of the indigo plant; madderwort, whose crushed roots produced the color red; and the mineral salts for the other colors, used on an industrial scale to color varnished ceramic tiles and fabrics.

As in the case of pottery, dyers' districts came into being just outside the town limits. Their marvellous extracts have proved to be perfect, and are still as luminous and brilliant a thousand years later!

Another practical contribution of chemistry to Islamic crafts: distilleries, using the first rudimentary stills to extract the juices of aromatic substances: rose, jasmine, lilac, violet, carnation, narcissus, animal musk, aromatic resins of myrrh.

A draper, from an early miniature.

These extracts were commonly used in the composition of perfumes, toilet waters, pastries and also of soaps which were being produced on a large scale.

Baghdad was the capital of this luxury industry.

As in the case of gardens and *objets d'art,* we are dealing here with a fringe of total production which deliberately involved the quest for a degree of sophistication hitherto unknown in Islam. At any rate it did much to popularize in the Mediterranean basin the unreal and glowing image of a fascinating Arabia of the *Thousand and One Nights.*

Weaving

The development of weaving workshops paralleled the arrival of textile plants brought back from conquests and produced by intensive cultivation: Turkish and Syrian cotton, Egyptian hemp Asian silk.

Despite Mohammed's prohibition of the wearing of silk garments, which were felt to be too luxurious and too lavish, the growing of silk was one of the major successes of Islam and proof of its wonderful capacity for adaptation. Having brought the first mulberry bushes back from China, they planted them throughout the regions with a subtropical climate (the Caspian Sea, for example); and, despite the complexity of the techniques involved, they set up silkworm farms in all parts of Tabaristan (now Mazanderan). Within a few years Muslim silk, which was fine and particularly well woven, invaded the market from the Indus to Spain.

It may not be commonly known that it takes a ton of mulberry leaves to feed one ounce of worms, from which 130 pounds of cocoons, yielding 6.5 pounds of silk thread, can be obtained. In other words, thirty mulberry bushes are needed to produce 6.5 pounds of silk! And that involved using complex, demanding and not always very reliable technology. The sheer magnitude of the effort made by Muslim

silkworm cultivators thus becomes apparent.

Other luxury woven products included fabrics sewn with gold and silver thread, gold brocades and carpets, all of which were being exported to many countries, even to Japan, as early as the 10th century!

Carpets were originally the basis furnishing of the Bedouin tent. They were woven or rather 'knotted' by the women of the family—since in fact the technique involved making a knot by hand around the woolen threads which made up the warp. The finer and closer the knots were, the more valuable, brilliant and solid the carpet would be. Only certain carpets, known as *kilim,* were woven like a fabric.

Carpet-making is still a highly traditional craft, which even today remains in the hands of family workshops using ancestral methods. Even the factories which are coming into being in so many places keep the motifs, if not the techniques, which were originally used. In the hamlets and in the tents, weaving continues much as before: first of all the loom has to be loaded with the threads of the warp; then comes the choice of a decorative theme and the dyeing of the wool: indigo leaves for blue, madderwort roots or cochineals for red, henna leaves for orange, saffron or sumac wood for yellow, buckthorn berries for green; iron oxide produced black but eventually spoilt the wool; nut barks made it possible to achieve the different shades of brown.

Decorative motifs in the Middle East were always geometric, while in Iran, which was more influenced by the proximity of the Far East, they tended to be floral. We find in them, mixed with traditional lozenges and triangles, interwoven stylized flowers and the ritual elements of oriental symbolism such as the cypress, the traditional 'tree of life'.

Recently the makers of the most commonly used type of small prayer mat have begun to depict on them the most famous sanctuaries of Islam (Jerusalem, Mashad, Qom) and even—despite the Koranic prohibition of such things—an image of the Prophet himself, complete with halo, just like Jesus Christ!

High quality carpets, which are often made on small vertical looms, on the basis of traditional patterns, may contain as many as ten thousand knots per fifteen square inches; this shows the extent to which the fibers are packed together by the heavy curry-combs.

Nowadays only the workshops in the small villages, and particularly those of the nomads, still preserve intact their centuries-old technique, which gives their products their peculiar brilliance and longevity.

Huge formal carpets and humble individual prayer mats alike have borne for centuries the prestigious name of their place of origin, which has its peculiar style, preferred motifs and dominant color.

A Tabriz, a Shiraz a Kirman or a Naïn have done more for the renown of Islam than many an official ambassador.

Mechanical industries

Though less well known, the mechanical industries also have many wonderful products to their credit: mechanical clocks from Damascus and Baghdad, capable of counting both hours and years. Watermills which could grind cereals by means of the force of the current: there was a huge one at Baghdad which operated a hundred mills, while the one at Mossul could grind fifty tons of grain a day.

The wind was sometimes substituted for the water as the power source for these mills: in Sistan, an eastern province of Iran, the wind turned curious vertical mills driven by drums.

The crafts and industries of Islam were comprehensive, rich and original moreover, they were the driving force behind an increasingly prosperous trade.

Merchants with their characteristic scales.

Trade

Before Mohammed the great trails linking the Far East to the Egean Sea had already been in existence for a long time, but they avoided Arabia, which was too far out of the way and too poor to be of any commercial interest.

The only activity in which the caravans were involved was the transit of merchandise entrusted to the Bedouins by their rich neighbors (Syria, Persia, Palmyra, Petra) for transport directly across the desert of Arabia, thus connecting the Persian Gulf and Aden to the Syro-Palestinian shores of the Mediterranean by the most direct route.

But from the 9th century onwards all the land and sea routes between the Far East and the Mediterranean were in Arab hands or under Arab control.

It is not possible to state exactly the volume of this trade, but it must have been considerable.

The caravans

Routes between the various regions, which had been known since the earliest times, were greatly influenced by the facts of geography. It was along these routes that all trade proceeded; indeed they are still today the main arteries of the Arabian region.

They were trails for pack animals, and not roads for wheeled vehicles such as those built by the Romans. They were used throughout the year by caravans of camels. Since the fertile and productive regions were separated by vast stretches of desert or mountains, an animal that was both

The defensive citadel-like appearance of the caravanserais show how unsafe the trade routes were: were it not for these 'fortified hotels' the merchandise would have stood no chance of ever getting to its destination.

The caravanserais were officially the property of the state, while the caravans were made up, just like a modern ship, by rich merchants who thus owned a 'fleet' of camels and camel-drivers.

It has been estimated that the profit made by the owners of these convoys which were strung out over the endless trails linking East to West was equivalent to fifty per cent of the value of the merchandise transported.

The classical silk route, from Samarkand to the Mediterranean, via Rey (Teheran) and Baghdad, was the most famous of the international trade routes.

But there were many others connecting the towns of the Far East to the Egean, or simply the major metropolitan centers of Islam to each other. In fact the network of caravan trails was practically as dense as their modern successors; both of them follow the same ancient routes.

Apart from the caravanserais there was another structure supporting these commercial migrations: hostelries for the care of the sick; fortified points to watch over and protect the trails; and a whole string of wells, fountains and bridges which helped make the journey safer if not more comfortable.

The sea lanes

While the overland routes were being organized in this way, the sea lanes had been developed to the point where they offered them competition. From the Muslim ports of the Persian Gulf (Bassorah, Barheim, Aden, Siraf, Kish), Islamic vessels sailed to Madagascar, Mozambique, India, Indonesia and China; they returned laden with valuable cargoes of ivory, spices, wood, grey amber, fabrics and even lions!

tough and undemanding was obviously needed. The camel, which could carry as much as 650 pounds for 60 miles a day without either food or drink was clearly the ideal solution.

The speed of the caravans did not exceed three miles an hour for a twelve hour day.

Every evening these caravans would stop overnight at a caravanserai, a genuine desert hotel with accomodation for both men and beasts, safe behind tall walls which protected the merchandise being transported. In a large inner courtyard surrounded by cells the camels were unloaded while the caravan drivers shared out the rooms amongst themselves after a meal in the communal parts—kitchen and dining room. The heavy gates were shut at nightfall.

This merchandise then had to be sent by caravans overland to the Mediterranean and Europe.

A large mercantile fleet was obviously indispensable for such an enterprise. It consisted of solidly built wooden vessels, the sail-powered boutres and junks.

Quite early on, two ports achieved pre-eminence in this commercial network: Siraf, on the Persian coast of the Gulf, which had a virtual monopoly of trade with India and China; and Aden, on the southern coast of Arabia, which was in a privileged situation for trade with Egypt, the Red Sea and East Africa, and also, through Suez and Alexandria, with the great commercial centers of Europe: Genoa, Pisa, Florence and Venice.

In the 10th century an earthquake destroyed Siraf; its inhabitants then resettled on the island of Kish, which soon become a miniature mercantile republic not unlike the Genoa and Venice of later centuries.

It took a month to sail from Arabia to India, and three more from there to China, as navigation was based on coastal routes. It was also greatly aided by the lighthouses which were situated along the way and by the emergence of new instruments: the compass, for finding one's exact position; the astrolab, for taking bearings; lights, to avoid collisions; sounding-lines for the measurement of depth.

The only real problem facing navigation was the pirates who lay in wait along the rocky coasts. It is less widely known that the Empire also made use of inland waterways to link the provinces to each other.

Few rivers lend themselves to such navigation, but those that do were used to the utmost: the Oxus, the Indus, the Tigris as far as Baghdad, and the Euphrates, which joined Syria to the Persian Gulf.

The thousands of canals which criss-crossed southern Mesopotamia supported intense activity in the region of Bassorah; indeed Chatt-al-Arab, formed by the confluence of the Tigris and the Euphrates,

The proud and astonishing buildings of the Atlas seem to be inspired by the contours of the natural setting in which they were built.

was crowed with travelers and merchandise. The craft used included a kind of fast gondola, the 30-foot long boutre, a curious circular vessel made of inflated sheepskins and also heavy Chinese-style junks.

The 'mail'

One internal consequence of such a dense trade network was the development of a kind of postal service linking the main cities of the Empire and relaying commercial messages and private mail.

Using meharis, horses or fast boats, it took twenty-four hours to make the round-trip journey between Mossul and Baghdad or Bassorah and Baghdad—a remarkable accomplishment when one thinks about it. Messages could even be transmitted by light signals and homing pigeons. They were sealed with wax and carriage was paid by the addressee on delivery.

A caste of bankers and merchants

Mohammed himself had accepted trade as necessary for the conquests which he had planned, since it was in fact the only way of bringing money into the coffers of Medina.

This trend was increased under the first caliphs and became fully organized during the Omayad period.

The moral code of Allah forbade only speculation and embezzlement, and allowed profits which were, after all, the very lifeblood of expansion.

International trade and wholesale business were in the hands of big merchants, particularly Jews or Armenians, since the Arabs considered these activities as beneath the dignity of their birth and religion.

Gradually an economic cartel came into being, consisting of bankers and merchants, which was so powerful that it lent money to vizirs and constituted a state within a state during the Abassid period.

This control of trade and finance gave converted 'foreigners' access to the highest posts in the state, and even to the caliphate which eventually found itself in a helpless

position, squeezed between the army and the merchants.

Such rising prosperity was possible only due to a strong currency.

Currency

At the time of Mohammed there was virtually no currency at all. The Arabs very soon had to make their first coins on the basis of those in use in conquered lands.

The models used were, in particular, the coins of Byzantium and Sassanid Persia. Under the Omayyads Islamic currency was being minted without any problems.

Transactions were conducted with three types of coin: a silver coin, the *dirham;* a gold coin, the *dinar;* and a copper coin for small purchases.

As in modern times, their value varied in the light of the international situation and the state of the harvests. They were usually weighed for major transactions, though certain unscrupulous merchants tended to scrape away here and there so as to accumulate a few ounces of silver or gold.

Arab coins have been found along all the trade routes they used, not only in the Orient but also in Europe, as far north as the shores of the Baltic and Scandinavia!

In other words, the trade of the known medieval world was in the hands of the Arabs; this commercial expansion was most certainly related to the extraordinary spread of Islam, even in non-occupied countries, merely through contacts, trade and prestige.

For example, there were eighty million Muslims in China and ten mosques in Peking.

But in the 7th century, Islam, which had originally been built on an idea which could be described as 'socialist', or at least as egalitarian, among all the faithful, led to a form of capitalism concentrated in the hands of a small number of merchants and financiers, as a result of the prodigious rise in the volume of Arab production and international trade.

Below: the marvelous ceiling of a room in the Alhambra, Granada.   Right: enameled glass lamp, 14th century (Islamic Museum, Cairo).   Following pages: ornamental motifs from a mosque at Kairouan and a window of a building in the same town; finely wrought plates; ceramics from the Ottoman period, powder boxes of copper; the domes of the mosque of Sultan Ahmed, at Istanbul and the mosque of Cordova.

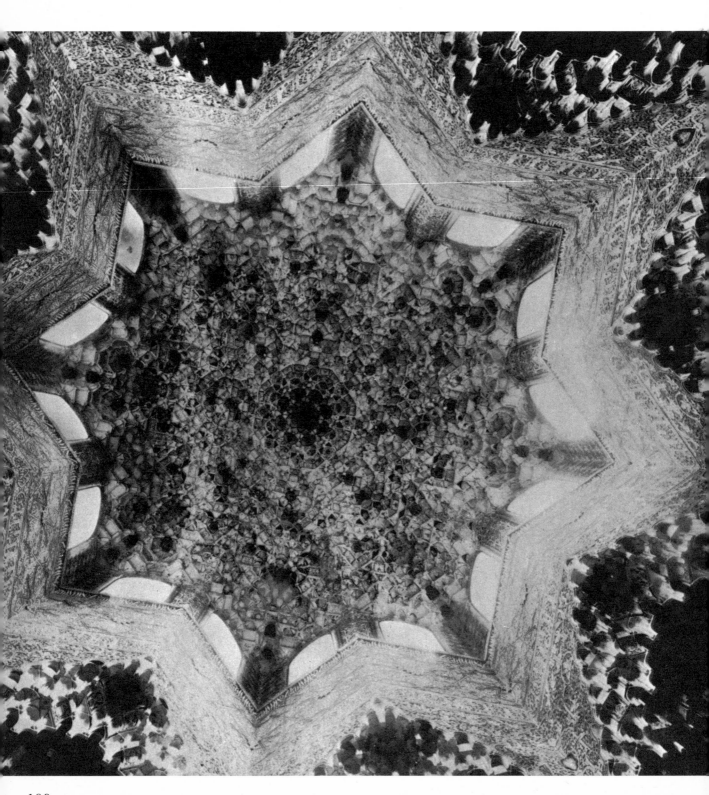

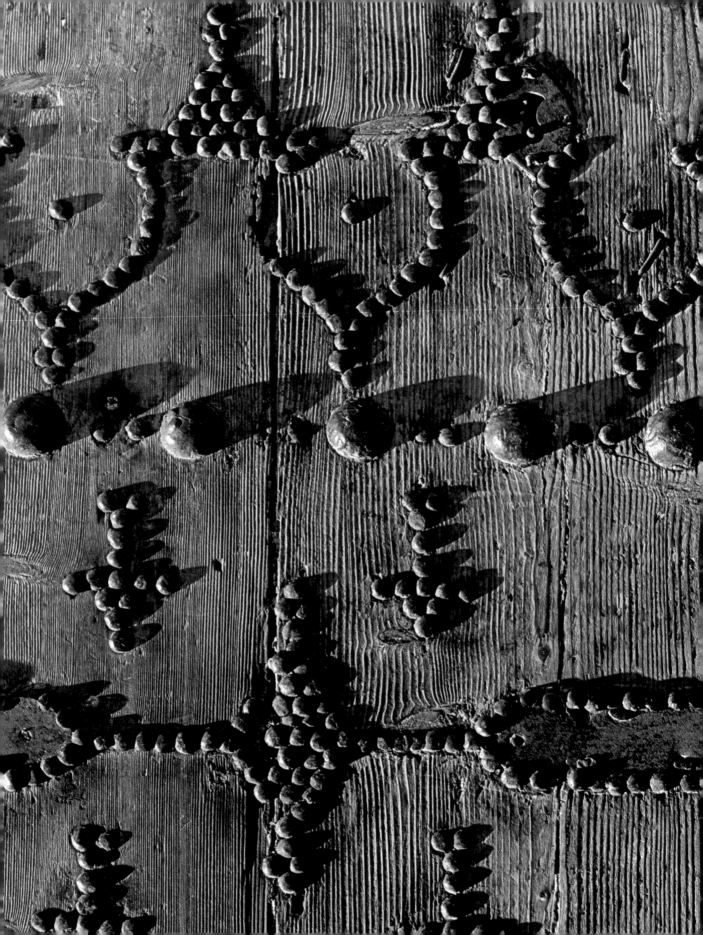

5. SCIENCES, LITERATURE AND THE ARTS

The sciences: practical and utilitarian

At the dawn of Islam the Koran, the sacred book, was the sole source of all intellectual inspiration.

The *Ulemas* who interpreted it represented at the time the entire body of orthodox Muslim knowledge and thinking.

But the conquest of Byzantium greatly impressed the conquerors by opening to them a world different from theirs, one containing a wealth of fascinating knowledge.

Muslim intellectuals then began to absorb this knowledge and to assimilate the arts with the same ardor that the Bedouin cavalry had applied to the creation of the Empire. In this vast venture of recovering the knowledge of antiquity, the Greeks were the first masters of the Arabs, who had the main works of the ancient philosophers and scholars translated into their knowledge; then they gradually set about learning Greek, Latin and Spanish, thus acquiring the key to the classical thinking which had preceded them.

This phase of compilation and study was completed in the 10th century.

But the Arabs were not content to merely ingest this mass of learning; having first assimilated it, they then proceeded to modify and enrich it with the inner fire of their mystical enthusiasm and their imagination.

They also disseminated it by means of a spectacular expansion of the number of madrasahs and public libraries which they

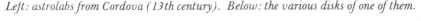

Left: astrolabs from Cordova (13th century). Below: the various disks of one of them.

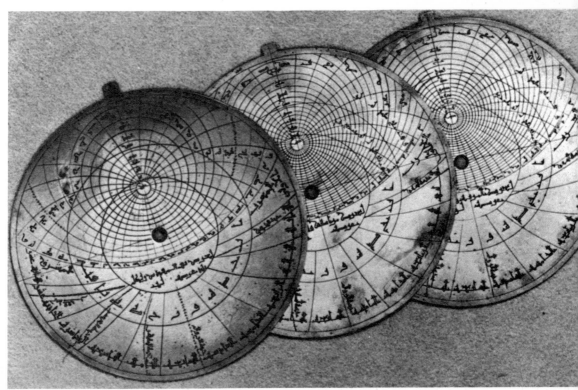

built in all the towns of the Islamic world. However, even though they respected the Greek masters they scrutinized them carefully and criticized them in the light of their own experience.

The original element in Muslim learning was its practical and utilitarian aspect.

The Greeks were abstract intellectuals, and the Arabs ingenious practitioners. On the theoretical knowledge which they had received they super-imposed experimentation and observation—thus frequently changing ancient knowledge by making possible its practical application.

It was to take another thousand years for our European Middle Ages to reach that stage of scientific experimentation.

Islam gathered the heritage of the ancient world, but it was no passive intermediary; once its intellectual enthusiasm had succeeded in amalgamating the Greek and oriental civilizations, it was a modified body of scientific knowledge that was later transmitted to Europe.

They studied the ancient texts, compared them, criticized them and checked them against experimentation and observation, the result being a very practical science which was quite unlike the abstractions of the ancient world.

The three greatest universities of Islam, the crucibles of that transformation, were Baghdad, Cairo and Cordova. Science and philosophy became more and more highly developed and independent at those centers of learning—and increasingly suspect in the eyes of the theocratic state.

Mathematics

The Western world believes it is using 'Arabic' numerals, though in fact the system of numbering of Islam is Hindu in origin, even though the words 'cipher' and 'zero' are Arabic. This system entered Europe in the 12th century, and was an immense step ahead by comparison with Roman figures, being much more practical for mathematical calculations.

Algebra is a perfect example of the way Islam transformed the knowledge which it had received. The word itself is Arabic, though the mathematical principle is ancient and was known to the authors of Greek antiquity.

But in the 9th century, Mohammed Ben Musa wrote a *Treatise of Popular Algebra* which greatly disseminated a method which was to set in motion of process of revolutionizing world science.

Similarly and even more practically, the calculation of volume and surfaces was given expression in definitive geometric and arithmetic formulas.

Trigonometry elaborated its basic theorems which are still in force; moreover, the ancient basis for the application of algebra to geometry has been confirmed and broadened.

Astronomy

Just as philosophy had a hard time shaking off science and religion, so also astronomy, although it was the first beneficiary of mathematical progress, could not easily rid itself of associations with astrology.

Originally, however, Abu-i-Wafa and Ab Battan d'Harran, as well as Ibn Yunus of Egypt continued the work of Ptolemy, even establishing the first catalogue of stars and discovering the principle of the astrolab. Amadjur and his son (833-933) established new astronomical tables and determined the latitude of Baghdad to within ten minutes.

Ali-ar-Bashman (903-936) wrote his *Book of the Stars* in which he portrayed all the known constellations by superimposing on them the animal or human forms which they retain to this day.

In the year 1000 Al Birani wrote an *Astronomical Encyclopedia* which discusses the possibility that the Earth might rotate around the Sun—long before Tycho Brahe—and drew the first maps of the sky, also using stylized animals to depict the constellations.

Like many others, the Islamic peoples moved easily from astronomy to astrology. Below: engraving taken from a Treatise on the Constellations *(15th century). Right: astrological figures from an early manuscript.*

Arab astronomical thinking was therefore closer to Copernicus than to Ptolemy.

The Baghdad school dominated astronomy for seven centuries, from 750 to 1450, its apogee occurring during the reign of Harun-al-Rashid and his son Mamun: from Asia to the Atlantic, the Muslim Empire was covered with observatories and specialized schools: Samarkand, Damascus, Cairo, Fez, Toledo Cordova, to mention only the most famous.

This was the time when studies were made of the equinoxes and the planets, and when the angle of the ecliptic was calculated to within a few degrees of the accuracy of the modern reading.

The Abassid decadence and the collapse of Baghdad meant that the torch of science and astronomy passed to Cairo, which had been separated from the Abassid Caliphate since the 10th century.

Next it was the turn of Spain and Cordova. Unfortunately all the Arabic manuscripts there were destroyed during the Christian reconquest.

In 1080 Arzachel studied the precession of the equinoxes and the apogee of the Sun and built astronomical clocks.

One wonders whether the Spanish astronomers had not even anticipated Kepler and Copernicus in the discovery of the elliptical movement of the planets and the Earth.

Their work was 'borrowed' by European scholars: the *Astronomical Tables* of Alfonso X are in fact a compilation of Arab elements.

They unquestionably mastered the measurement of time by means of sun dials and the making of perfect astrolabs, thus greatly facilitating navigation.

The applied sciences

Observation and experimentation had, as their immediate corollary, the development of the practical applications of mathematics and the fundamental sciences.

— *Physics:* Most of their works on theo-

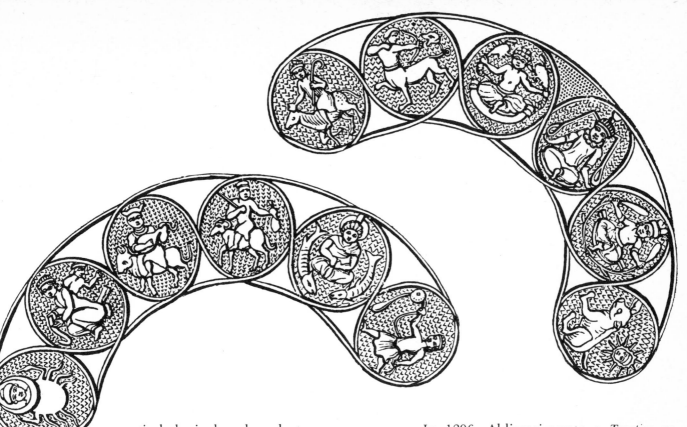

retical physics have been lost.

But we are familiar with their utilitarian applications, which were put to use in the 10th century and later.

Optics developed considerably, with the discovery of the properties of lenses and mirrors and the establishment of the laws of reflected images.

The treatise on optics written by Al-Hazen, which was used by Kepler, was the point of departure of the construction of magnifying glasses and telescopes, and really marked the beginning of practical astronomy and the observation of the stars.

— *Mechanics:* few instruments have survived to modern times; however, the ingenuity and the technical skills of the Arabs was at the origin of exceptional devices which applied the theories of their scientists.

The astrolab, some examples of which are genuine works of art, the compass, which was invented by the Chinese but perfected and disseminated by the navigators of Islam a century before Europe, are among the most useful and most spectacular of their instruments.

We should also mention the still, invented for the distillation of plants, and the hydraulic pump.

In 1206, Aldjazari wrote a *Treatise on Automats,* recording all the mechanical processes which were to be the point of departure of watchmaking and most of the machines which existed before the coming of steam and electricity.

A perfect mastery of metallurgy and the use of steel made all of these accomplishments more easily possible.

— *Chemistry:* in this sphere the heritage of Greece and the ancient world in general was rather slight.

In fact the Arabs had virtually to invent the whole of modern chemistry.

Though they were bogged down in alchemy, they nonetheless discovered, as early as the tenth century, alcohol, nitric and sulfuric acids, silver nitrate and potassium.

Then they determined the specific weight of numerous bodies and mastered the technique of sublimation, crystallization and distillation.

Geber (Latinized form of Jabir Ibn Hayan) the famous Iranian chemist who died in 804 at Tous, in Khorassan, was the father of all these discoveries, which were recorded in an encyclopedia and numerous treatises covering two thousand works which were the Bible of European chemists

of the 18th century, particularly of Lavoisier.

These works led naturally to the following uses: tinctures and their applications in tanning and textiles; distillations of plants of flowers, the origin of perfumes and therapeutic pharmacy; and of course gunpowder, a powerful instrument of military superiority which Islam possessed long before the West.

— *Geography:* the need for trade relations with their neighbors obliged the Arabs to know the world of their day as accurately as possible.

The first 'explorer geographers' were thus those anonymous merchants who, covering the length of all the trails, visited the towns and later wrote accounts of their travels. For example, in 851 Sulei-

man, a merchant who had set out from Siraf, wrote the first known work about China.

In 740 Nadhar, of Bassorah, wrote the first treatise of geography, presenting all this borrowed knowledge in a single work.

Soon the historians and philosophers themselves also began traveling to discover the world. In the 9th century (about 880), Masoudi devoted twenty-five years of his life to travels about the Islamic Empire, then producing a famous work, which was philosophical, historical and geographical in nature, *The Golden Meadows.*

In the 10th century Al-Istakhri wrote a *Book of the Countries,* which was a compilation of knowledge about the oriental world of his day.

It was soon completed, about 1150, by

The map of the known world, established in the 13th century by the famous geographer Edrisi.

a *Great Atlas,* by Al Idrissi, which contain ed maps of the sea lanes and overland routes between East and West.

The military took an interest in geography; about the year 1000, Ali Rouni accompanied King Mahmoud, his master, on his Indian campaign, and brought back a descriptive chronicle of the countries visited which is strongly reminiscent of the work of Joinville written as he followed Saint Louis.

In 1154 a certain Edrasi wrote a work on medieval Europe, Spain and Sicily.

In the 13th century, Aboud Hassan explored the coasts of the Maghreb in order to verify and complete the summary cartography of the Phenicians and ancient Egyptians.

In 1325, Ibn Batouah, who had set out from Tangiers, crossed North Africa, Syria, Mesopotamia and Iran and eventually reached India. He went on by sea as far as China, via Ceylon, Java and Sumatra.

In 1388, Al-Quzwini wrote his *Marvels of Creation,* a compendium of the geographical and naturalist knowledge of his day.

It can be said that by the end of the 14th century the known world had been perfectly explored and described by Arab travelers, who thus transmitted to Europe the revelation of the oriental world.

At the same time scientists had helped bring about a better understanding of the Earth by measuring the terrestrial meridian and publishing a series of studies of ethnography, sociology and physical geography. Maps of the coasts of the Mediterranean, the Indian Ocean and Red Sea were also drawn, on the basis of accounts written by navigators who had ranged all over the seas, from Gibraltar to Japan.

The natural sciences were also being developed; the first classifications of zoology were being made, and in 1280 Kazwiny wrote a large illustrated book about animals, reminiscent of the work of Buffon,

500 years later.

Mineralogy and even fossils had already been described and classified, and a *Treatise on Stones* by Avicenna summarized current knowledge about geology.

Medicine

Situated somewhere on the borders of science and philosophy, Arab medicine had derived its foundations from the work of the great doctors of antiquity, Hippocrates and Galien, who were translated into Arabic in 685 by Aaron.

Here again, however, the curiosity inherent in the Arab temperament transformed the medical knowledge of the Greeks, which was as theoretical as a philosophy, into an art. The observation and experimentation devoted to this end led to considerable and rapid progress not only in knowledge of diseases but also in their treatment. But it was not until the 16th century that the accomplishments of Arab medicine became widely known in Europe.

Rhazes (850-932) was both a doctor and a chemist; he taught medicine at Baghdad for fifty years. His was a revolutionary medicine in that it commented on and criticized the classical theories at the patient's bedside.

In this way, on the basis of sound anatomical knowledge and a perfect understanding of the ancient writings, there gradually came into being a clinical medicine which combined the first elements of semeiology and diagnosis.

Avicenna, who has already been mentioned in connection with philosophy, was one of the greatest doctors of Islam in the 12th century. For centuries his description of disorders was to be the Bible of the Middle Ages and the Renaissance, and was still consulted in the 18th century.

Hygiene, which was in itself something of a revolution, and physiology were elevated to their proper place for the first time.

Averroes, another philosopher of the 12th century, was also interested in physio-

ويلزيد من زياده شيئه طعمه لعند الاراد خلطا لعضو الطبيعيه جلدون ما هي هذا الذي اقشرت بعضها وحدث بعض خاصه حلطها
بعضان لهذين من احول لما هم جهده ان احدث الذي اقشرت بعضها وحدث بعض خاصه خلطها
ولهذا سمرت اليه نايه عرف ذار القوده على اي القرسه وان لطف الطعام عن
الاحساس اليه لاستوفاء الشريان انقرمار طبيعه على لقاد الطوسه فلاي القرسه وان لطف الطعام عن
الاحساس اليه لاستوفاء الشريان انقرمار طبيعه على لقاد الطوسه على باد وصفنا غشاء القرير حول الطعمه القريه ورحديث ان نفتح شرائع الطعين
لحم الخمس بامثال لها لاته لا لعنه اخشاء عفوذ الطوبه على باد وصفنا غشاء القرير حول الطعمه القريه ورحديث ان نفتح شرائع الطعين بها
يالنباس الصفاء والعود امضان بعون عراد من الام بلاموسط عضما بعضها لاته لفتح كله لعله البصر من نفسه
خالخت الحمسطن متوسط طبيعتها الطبيعيه الرم ودك هي الطوبه الزجاجه
لقربه الي البياس والصفنه الام فلذك صارت الطوبه الحليله باسه دع وعلى هذا المثال
لقيه الزجاجيه ليس بها الجرجوي معرفه فيها الي نصفها واما
الشبيهه بالسيخ اللتي تحوي هذه الطوبه الزجاجيه فانها

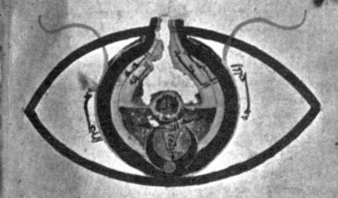

والمبتدى بالاخبار عن ما فعل وعدد الرطوبات والطبقات اللتي وضعناها
بعض الشباش وكوها ومنشها ومواضعها واركنت لحق ذلك ان يصف احبارك

logy and left a curious treatise on poisons and fevers. For him also, hygiene was fundamental, and the notion of the prevention of diseases which it was not yet possible to cure showed remarkable philosophical and medical wisdom. Washing, the prohibition of alcohol and wine, a frugal and vegetable diet were all religious prescriptions which were put to work in the service of hygiene and medical prophylaxis in medieval Islam.

In parallel with medicine, surgery was beginning to make progress.

Abulcassis (913-1013?), of Cordova, a professor at the medical school of Zahara, laid its foundations in the form of a 30-volume medical encyclopedia which remained unchallenged for five centuries. It was not until the 15th century that two treatises on surgery were published: that of the Turk Charaf-ed-Din, and that of the Arab Abi Ibn.

Oriental surgery appeared to be divided into two groups of techniques: cauterization and bleeding surgery.

Cauterization consisted in the application of a red-hot iron to the diseased area.

This method, which had been in use in ancient Greece, was applied in abundance in Islam, regardless of the nature of the disorder to be treated. It might conceivably have been some kind of acupuncture.

There were abundantly illustrated treatises which showed in detail how cauterization was to be used in fifty-six diseases ranging from sprains to pneumonia!

Bleeding surgery was more feared and less commonly practised, but it was already quite varied. Here again, Abulcassis, the greatest surgeon until the Middle Ages, set the rules for dissection and hemostasis by ligature, procedures which made proper operations possible: it was, of course, hemorrage which posed the greatest problem and risked getting completely out of hand in the surgery of the day.

Minor surgery was common: vessical probes, the incision of abscesses, punctions for ascitis and hydrocelitis, and, as one might expect, the universal remedy of bleeding.

At a higher level small sub-cutaneous tumors were treated, arrowheads could be removed and wounds sutured.

Islamic surgeons even ventured to remove tonsils, carry out amputations, close hernias and treat varicose veins by means of staggered transcutaneous ligatures.

Tracheotomies, laparotomies and even intestinal sutures with hemp thread were all performed, but only exceptionally.

The nascent art of dentistry was not confined to the extraction of diseased teeth, but even tackled remedial techniques by the use of artificial teeth made of bone and attached to the healthy teeth with steel wire.

This restless quest for new knowledge and technology was made possible by two innovations: first, by the existence, in each major town, of hospitals; these were the *bimaristans,* which assembled the patients in groups, but in which attempts at hygiene were powerless against the cramped and dirty conditions which are so conducive to the spread of disease.

Secondly, by the use of instruments (scalpel, tongs, scissors, forceps) and minor medical supplies (splints, plasters, compresses, hemp or steel thread, cotton, etc.) which enabled doctors to venture into new methods.

In actual fact the results of any treatment involving bleeding must have been terrifying, because of the absolute absence of antiseptics and the complete ignorance of the role of germs in the transmission of infectious diseases.

A philosophical detail of some social importance: the incurable cases were totally neglected; nothing was done even to help them over their last moments of life.

Knowledge of parasites, however, was advancing: sarcoptes of the intestine, the so-called Medina worm, and others. Some very special diseases such as homophilia had been studied: the doctors of Islam knew that it was passed down within the family, though they had no notion of genetic heredity.

A major practical accomplishment was made in the treatment of fractures by reduction and contention. Since plaster was still unknown the doctor used splints consolidated by strips of fabrics soaked in egg white which were thus made both heavier and stronger.

Another innovation was the beginning of systematic medical therapy, which had been made possible and current by a knowledge of the medicinal plants from which it was possible to extract syrups, elixirs, extracts, lotions, potions, ointments and plasters, by grinding or distillation.

Commonly used plants included rhubarb, senna, nux vomica, cherry stems and leeks.

Despite all these efforts, the death rate among babies, children and the aged was enormously high. Even so, the Arabs derived the maximum benefits from what they had available to them, given the absence of the crucial notion of germs, which was to be the next step forward, several centuries later.

This was because all other branches of fundamental knowledge—chemistry, physics and even philosophy—assisted the flowering of Islamic medicine making it the most curious, remarkable and imaginative of its period.

Libraries and the literary language

For half a millenium, from 700 to 1200, Islam dominated the world by virtue of the power and attraction of its radiant and original civilization. The vehicle for this artistic and intellectual presence was exactly the same as for trade.

The circulation of ideas, at first limited by the rarity of ancient parchments and Egyptian papyri, was revolutionized by the invention of paper—at first Chinese and then Arabic—and binding.

The coming of the book completely upset the cultural landscape of the world. Books were expensive and rare to begin with, it is true; but they did enable the cultivated public to have direct contact with the works of poets, philosophers and scholars.

All available works were soon assembled in the libraries which flourished in all the towns of the Empire, such was the Arab appetite for learning and dreams.

Until the time of Mohammed libraries were rare and reserved for a university or religious elite: at Samarkand and Balk they were in the hands of Buddhist monks. At Jondi-Shahpur, in Sassanid Persia, a university which was famous throughout the Orient in the 6th century welcomed and trained doctors, scholars and philosophers.

At Alexandria the most famous of them all contained the quintessence of contemporary learning.

Islam's contribution was the democratization of knowledge and the dissemination of written works. From the 9th to the 12th century a full-scale passion for books came into being. Poets became increasingly well known and popular. Historians, geographers, scholars and philosophers were all on the move, discovering the world.

This was the great intellectual awakening of Islam. Each mosque had its library, some of which were huge and prestigious. At the Al-Kazar mosque there were 600,000 works; a similar number were to be found

at Damascus and Baghdad.

Even the intellectuals had lavish private libraries; moreover, they represented three per cent of Islamic society in the 12th century.

A story was told of a famous doctor who had to forgo moving to the court at Bokhara as it would have taken four hundred camels to transport his books!

The ordinary people, who were left out of all this intellectual ferment, managed to catch up to some extent by tasting some of the sap of intellectual revolution while listening to the itinerant poets and storytellers.

In the open air, in the coffee-houses, indeed everywhere, crowds would gather to listen to poems and legends, stories and apologias such as the people were fond of hearing.

Originally most written works were texts from antiquity, transmitted by Christians in the Syriac tongue. At an early date, however, the Arabic language besides its role as the ideal vehicle for the Islamic faith and the cement of Arabism, in the political sense of the term, also became the instrument of Muslim civilization.

All works were thus translated into Arabic, the official language of knowledge, creativity and business throughout the Empire.

There was the written language, belonging to the Semitic group, quite close to Hebrew and very different from the Indo-European languages, and also a spoken language which was abundantly diversified in dialects which varied from one country and often from one province to another.

The first written language, Kufic, had no vowels—which made it very difficult to pronounce and, particularly, to transcribe.

In the 8th century, therefore, the Arabic language was transformed by the addition of signs indicating the place and nature of the missing vowels. Even that did not avoid the large numbers of phonetic transpositions used to spell the same words in different ways.

By the 9th century, however, there was an Arabic dictionary in twenty volumes (by Ibn-Seid) and numerous syntactical works.

The ordinary people could not write; and—apart from the intellectuals—the use of writing was monopolized by a body of scribes not unlike those of ancient Egypt. They gave rise to a privileged caste, indispensable for the conduct of relations between the state and private individuals and greatly feared by the civil servants of the day.

Literary creativity soon found a marvelous medium for inspiration in the imagination, enthusiasm and sensitivity of Arab mysticism.

In this sense the first literary work is the Koran, whose formal perfection was, in the eyes of Mohammed, proof of its divine origin.

Islamic literature is highly original, essentially allegorical, sensorial and poetic. Just as the Arabs were imbued with the scientific contribution of pre-Islamic antiquity, so also, in the contrary direction, the modes of expression and thought peculiar to that same antiquity were alien to them. The Greek is a cerebral being skilled at handling abstractions, whereas the Arab is essentially a sensitive instinctive creature.

Poetry

This was the literary form which best corresponded to the people's need for refinement and illusion.

Borrowing Greek poetic meter, which was an intellectual mechanism, it tempered it and also invented rime, providing a musical setting for the phrase.

There had originally been a 'poetry of the desert', long before Mohammed. This form, which had been purely Bedouin and based on oral tradition, was recited in the tents and the villages by storytellers with

prodigious memories.

It was a chivalrous kind of poetry, relating the exploits of heroes and warriors, or exalting the beauty of the landscapes which the Bedouin crossed during their long migratory travels under the stars. This first form of poetry was a rhythmic modulation the *Radjiz,* a primitive harmony singing of the glory and the life of the tribes, which scanned to the rhythm of the camels' footsteps.

A more elaborate, more literary form was the *Qasica,* a genuine rhythmic poem, in rimed feet, which told of the passion of men, the greatness of Allah and the conquests of Islam.

Its traditional form was very precise: a long litany of between six and a hundred verses, usually with a single rime, having always the same number of feet calculated on the basis of a strict meter of long and short feet, and divided into three parts: prologue, narrative and eulogy. This made it possible to dedicate it to some powerful person in order to obtain protection or advantages.

Quite unlike this rough, popular and naive poetry, there was a poetry of the towndwellers: more highly colored, lighter and quite openly amorous and even bacchic—curiously for a society with such rigorous moral precepts and a prohibition of wine.

It was particularly common in the towns; Mohammed took a dim view of it because of its superficial, licentious character.

It was also possible for poetry to be a sort of utilitarian mode of expression: the chief of the tribe would become its spokesman, addressing some high personage in rimed verse in order to secure some benefit for his clan.

At any rate, it was always allegorical, symbolic and flowery. The arabesque was already a common feature of speech, long before it made its first appearance on walls.

There were, accordingly, few poets who

could write verse about their own personal inner emotions, rather than those of a famous hero or one of the traditional themes: women and love.

And there was a reason for this. It was impossible to live by one's writings, and only those works which praised the dignitaries of the court or the state could generate the glory and the money needed to sustain a regular literary production, which was clearly a precarious business; in other words, even the famous were often a stone's throw away from ruin.

With the exception of certain strong poetic personalities, and the archaic poetry of the traditionalists, all the rest was merely a superficial courtly poetry, totally circumstantial in nature.

Yet poetry was one of the most subtle gifts the Arabs have given to the world.

The theater had no appeal for their oriental sensibility; the novel did not exist; and prose was reserved almost exclusively for scientific works.

When, by chance, a literary work happened to be in prose, it was always a collection of short stories or of anecdotes that could be easily recited.

And to make them more agreeable to the audience, crude rimes were devised for the ends of paragraphs, based on assonance.

There were poetic competitions, not only at court but also among the ordinary people; the winner of these veritable literary jousting matches between the tribes used to have their names inscribed in letters of gold on the walls of the Kaaba, at least before the coming of Mohammed.

The Prophet was powerless to stop this popular entertainment. For a time, however, he did stigmatize frivolous and bacchic poetry, which had to wait until the time of the lavish courtly life of the Omayyads and the soft decadence of the Abassids before making its appearance again.

Poems were often read to a musical accompaniment, clearly an ancestor of the Spanish *Romancero*.

Copyright was obviously unknown. The poets lived only by means of capricious and highly unreliable patronage in high places, or from poorly paid work as copyists.

On the other hand once a poet became famous his writings were disseminated and known throughout the Muslim world, being brought to the notice not just of the nobles at court but also of the ordinary people, who were always anxious to find new dreams.

From the host of more or less anonymous poets, a few names have come down to us, those of the ones who were most famous, most talented or best placed at court:

Aby Nuwas (747-815), a Persian poet at the court of the great Harun-al-Rashid. Melancoly, libertine, disillusioned.

Aby Atahiya (825). Popular poet of religiosity and death.

Said Ibn Jadi (897). Both warrior and troubadour; his themes were war and love.

Al-Moutanabi (915-965). One of the great lyric poets, who sang the merits of the great and of princes. A magician with words.

Al-Maari (937). Syrian of Aleppo. Blind, he disdained courtly poetry, eschewed the kind of poetry that praised the deeds of kings and lived poorly. His satirical, skeptical and reform-minded verses contain much criticism of the society in which he lived.

However, from amongst all this morass of works there emerged some really talented prose-writers:

Al-Djaliz. The author, in 868, of the *Book of the Misers,* the *Book of the Animals,* and the *Book of Expression;* he inaugurated the genre of the 'essay', taking psychological analysis and critical synthesis to great artistic heights.

Ibn-Abd-Rablih. In 940 he wrote a synthesis of contemporary knowledge in the form of a work of popularization which

was both historical and practical, seasoned with humorous anecdotes to bring it within reach of the people.

At-Tawkidi. In 1023 he wrote satirical portraits of the vizirs.

But the most famous of all these works is without a doubt the unique collection known as the *Thousand and One Nights,* which was for a long time the only face of the Orient known in the West.

This work is a compilation which was constantly being enriched: the original core of the first tale was an Indo-Persian creation of the 10th century, to which were added, with each passing century, the contributions of successive storytellers.

Under the gentle mask of a poetico-fantastic narrative, this work provides us with a picture of the customs of the period. This veritable *Summa* of oriental popular literature is a fabric of symbolism and conventions in which animals, women and refinement are all inter-mingled to produce a caricature of an elegant but artificial Arabism.

Another popular best-seller was the *Al-Maquamat,* written in the 12th century by a high official of Baghdad. It gives an account of the imaginary and exemplary adventures of Abu Zayd, a glib and crafty vagabond reminiscent of Figaro (only even more shameless and underhand) in a poetic language full of charm and fantasy.

Lastly, the famous *Golden Meadows,* written by Macoudi in the 10th century: this is a prototype of the grand epic tales inspired by mystical poetry and faith.

History

From the 7th century onwards we see the appearance of historical accounts, written in prose, which, despite their attempt to be objective, could not quite escape a certain enthusiastic and wild lyricism.

Mohammed Ibn Ishak wrote in 763 a *Life of Mohammed* which was the first Arabic work to be published since the Koran.

Ibn Kutaïba (828-890) wrote an ambitious *History of the World* which gave an account of the origins and evolution of the Middle East, before and after the revolution of Islam.

Al Tabari (839-923): a Persian who died in Baghdad after forty years devoted to a *Chronicle of Kings and Apostles,* drafted without commentaries, in the form of a purely documentary and chronological encyclopedic compilation.

Al Masdi: died in exile in Cairo in 956. This great traveler was already considered as a subversive because of the philosophical conclusions he reached in his historical writings.

But, even though these works contain some interesting documents concerning the period, they are also a mishmash of loosely related anecdotes, lacking altogether the spirit of synthesis which is indispensable to the methodology of the true historian.

The tales

Quite as popular as poetry, the tales were one of the favorite modes of expression of the Arab soul. People used to meet everywhere, in coffee-houses, in tents or at court, to listen to these stories read by professional storytellers who were genuine troubadours of the short story. This was a form specially cultivated by the Arabs of Egypt.

Like poetry, their themes were love, chivalry, battles, religion, adventure. Only in prose.

With little regard for psychology, they dwelt mainly on the fantastic.

There were also fables and apologias, the metaphorical formulation of which lay at the origin of some our Western proverbs: 'The bush which produces the rose also produces the thorn'; 'associate with blacksmiths and you will get covered with soot, associate with a perfumer and you will smell sweet'; 'in a mouth which knows how to stay closed a fly will not enter'.

The public fondness for this popular form of sententious and moralizing wisdom, and also for tales of love and adventure, was the origin of what could be 'literature of entertainment'. It gave rise to a whole number of minor works, sometimes even libertine and pornographic, which periodically met with a vigorous puritanical response.

Philosophy

At the beginning of their civilization philosophy, in the sense of intellectual speculation, did not exist among the Arabs.

All they had was their powers of observation, their common sense and their personal experience of practical psychology.

The first translations of the Greek authors, Plato, Aristotle, Empedocles, Epicurus and other exponents of dialectics and thinking rapidly disseminated throughout the intellectual elite the reflections of ancient philosophy. However, progress in this field was slow, since it did not correspond to the frame of mind of the Arabs, which was more mystical and sensorial than abstract and cerebral.

Moreover, the few writers or poets who were drawn to the manipulation of ideas— a notion hitherto unknown in Islam—were greatly feared by the temporal and spiritual rulers on account of the danger they represented over the longer term to the traditional institutions and beliefs of Islam.

Even so, 'free thinking' was born of the first philosophical reflections of the Arabs: quite early on they accepted only the unity of God and the revealed character of the mission of the Prophet.

But they questioned the dogma and rites of Islam, making for the first time an essential distinction between, on the one hand, faith and belief which were highly personal and individual matters, and, on the other, religion and theocracy, which were artificial and contrived creations of the clerical hierarchy.

This analysis scandalized the disciplined believers and bigots, while spreading panic among the authorities, which did not hesitate to banish the authors of such subversive thoughts.

They were few in number, however, as philosophy merged, at the beginning, with the discovery of science, and was particularly a blend of thought and knowledge.

For that reason the first famous philosophers were scientists.

There are three names which are particularly well known in the West:

Avicenna (980-1037). Born at Bokhara and died in Iran, at Hamadan; he was above all one of the most famous doctors ever produced by Islam. But he also published a *Oriental Philosophy* and *Mystical Narratives* which place him in the tradition of Aristotle and the Neo-Platonic school.

Omar Khayyam (1050-1123). Born and died at Nishahpur, he was a disciple of Avicenna. His philosophical work was represented by collections of poems conveying a particular thesis, skeptical, pessimistic, irreverent and sacrilegious for the traditionalists of Islam.

They were prudently passed around in a covert manner so as to avoid adverse reactions from the religious authorities.

Averroes (1126-1198). Born at Cordova and died at Marrakesh, he spent his life between Andalusia and Morocco. He was the *cadi* of Seville and Cordova; he wrote the *Commentaries on Aristotle,* which were condemned by both Islam and the Christian church; in this work he developed his theory opposed to 'revealed' and unverifiable truths and in support of rational truths proved by science. This materialist and rationalist conception of a 'double truth' caused his works to be banned.

Architecture

The flowering of the arts, which paralleled that of literature and science, followed the explosion of Islam and the great

drive for expansion.

Their refinement greatly impressed the West, which was fascinated and spellbound by the originality, the magnificence and the elegance of Islamic architecture and decoration, which were among the more spectacular achievements of Muslim civilization.

As usual, it was religion, ever anxious to raise its sanctuaries to the skies, which lay behind this and most other manifestations of architectural progress.

It is in order to honor their gods, kings and dead that men build their finest monuments.

Architecture was thus the first, the most characteristic and the most spectacular product of Islam.

The *mosque* is the center and the symbol of Muslim religious life. It is there that the faithful go to pray and prostrate themselves before Allah. There is no single type of mosque, but several, which correspond to the habits and characteristics of each ethnic group and each region.

The Arab mosque is based traditionally on the floor plan of the house of Mohammed at Medina: a large rectangular courtyard, open to the sky, accessible by several entrances.

On each of the long sides facing each other there are two porticoes made of several rows of wooden columns. Opening onto the biggest of the covered porticoes were the rooms where the Prophet lived with his family and where he received pilgrims and disciples.

This plan recurs in Arab mosques, the finest example of which is that of Kairouan, where the living quarters are simply replaced by the prayer room, an immense room bristling with columns and padded with carpets. The space reserved for women is marked out by high grills made of carved wood, in a secluded, dark corner.

In the middle of the wall facing Mecca there is a narrow niche, the *mihrab,* corresponding to the apse of the church; next to it is a *nimbar,* the equivalent of the Christian pulpit.

The majestic originality of the mosque is due to its stark grandeur, the splendor of the marvelous decor woven onto its walls and the purity of the domes fashioned for the greater glory of Allah. A single minaret, equivalent to our belltower, is used to call the faithful to prayer.

On the other hand, the royal mosque of Isfahan is the prototype of the Iranian sanctuary, arranged around a huge central courtyard with a basin for ablutions.

But its originality lies in the presence, in the middle of each face, of an *iwan,* an essential architectural element peculiar to Iran. It is an immense vaulted niche, a hall with a high vaulted ceiling crowned with a semi-cupola. It is an intermediate space for transition between the courtyard and the prayer room.

The four iwans are thus situated facing each other, and, two by two, they create an axial symmetry characteristic of this type of mosque.

Whereas in the Arab world only the side of the courtyard facing Mecca has a prayer room, in Iran each of the four iwans leads to a room, bare or with columns. The one which is facing Mecca is still the most important, however; it is crowned with a principal dome and its entrance iwan is flanked by two tall minarets.

This principal prayer room is occupied by a forest of columns and contains a hollowed-out mirhab marking the mystical center of the structure.

Another interesting feature, the basin plays a dual role: ritual, in that it is used for the traditional ablutions; and also esthetic, since it serves as a mirror for the façades, thus creating a symmetry in space which generates breadth and majesty.

One last symbolic characteristic: the proportion of the buildings corresponds to numbers of gold, chosen in ratios of three,

four and five, which are those of the perfect triangle of Pythagoras, the sum of which is twelve, like the number of sacred imams of the Shiites.

As for Turkish mosques, they are noteworthy in that they have a single prayer room, placed in the center and crowned with a gigantic low dome, flanked by two, four or six minarets, very tall and very slender, which lend a great deal of refined elegance to the outline of the building.

This use of the dome is evidently reminiscent of Byzantium and doubtless has much to do with the demands of a harsher climate: the winters in Anatolia rule out vast courtyards open to the sky. The Blue Mosque of Suleiman, in Istanbul, is the finest illustration of this architectural conception.

All these mosques have one thing in common: the existence of a pool or monumental fountain in the center of the courtyard, for use in ritual ablutions; a profusion of columns made of wood or stone, smooth or twisted, probably a vestige of ancient influences; a very special type of arch, projecting and resting on slender columns with capitals; and in particular the use of 'stalactites', pitted in the form of beehives, an original architectural process devised by Arab architects in order to pass from the square to the circle and have a dome resting on a square base.

Having started out as a technical necessity, this solution became a decorative style characteristic of Islam.

The *madrasah:* these were the higher theological schools, and also the equivalent of our universities, because there was no more separation between religion and the state.

As the younger children learned to read in the Koran, the students discovered in these institutions the learning of their period, in a setting of serenity and harmony.

All of them are built on the same plan,

which is similar to that of the mosque. A courtyard enlivened by a garden and a pool, bordered on all sides by one or two floors of students' rooms not unlike the cells of Christian monks. A small prayer room invariably occupies the center of the side facing Mecca.

People used to meet there to pray, meditate and learn. Knowledge was dedicated and consecrated to Allah.

The madrasahs, which were very numerous, were grouped together in the older quarters, around the Great Mosque.

Some of them are included in the annexes of the mosques, thus adding even more to religious control over intellectual endeavors. Most of them are still in use, full of students wearing grey cloaks and white turbans.

Mausoleums. The tombs and mausoleums dedicated to the memory of the countless saints of Islam are very numerous, in both town and country.

They preserve the mortal remains, or at least the memory, of some local sage, usually unknown and anonymous.

There are only two types of such buildings, both of them set on a stone base containing a crypt: those with a square plan, crowned with a polygonal roof with four, six or eight panels; and the cylindrical ones which are covered with a conical roof.

Inside they contain a sarcophagus of carved stone or a funeral cage made of ornate wood. These are also remarkable for the harmony of their line and the elegance of their silhouette, which is usually enhanced by more or less refined decorative work.

Caravanserais. These are the quintessential type of functional and utilitarian architecture.

Spread out along the trails which linked the Mediterranean to the Indus, or serving the provinces of the Empire, they also were made on the same pattern: a huge courtyard where the camels were unloaded, surrounded by tiny bedrooms where the travelers would sleep in cramped conditions after a meal in one of the kitchens-cum-dining rooms which occupied each corner of the building. They were really peaceful and defensive citadels, which protected animals, people and merchandise against bandits.

Fonduks. These existed only in the bazaars of the older towns, where they provided accomodation for the merchants who could sleep there in cells surrounding the courtyard where their packages were piled up.

This building, which was both a hotel for business-people and warehouse for their merchandise, were perfectly typical of the Muslim civilization and are still in use today, at least as warehouses.

Hammams. These public baths are to be found in abundance throughout the older quarters and in rural areas; they are the transposition of the Roman thermal baths.

Ranging from the plain to the very lavish, they contained a succession of paved rooms covered with small domes illuminated by means of small portholes which let in the daylight.

The bather could choose between hot and cold baths, steamheated sweating rooms and resting rooms with divans. The baths of the Alhambra in Granada are an excellent example.

Palaces. With the mosques these were the jewels of the more prestigious architecture of Islam.

However, unlike the mosques, which were as brilliant as possible, the palaces usually had a rather dull and sober exterior, almost always disappointing.

But the marvels of art began inside, with the dizzying whirl of ceramics, interwoven stucco, inlaid wood and also the subtle art of the gardens, which echoed to the gentle splashing of water, miraculously domesticated for both beauty and comfort.

The Palace of Fin, in Iran, the Generalife, in Granada, the Alcazar of Seville are the most spectacular vestiges of that oriental refinement, a reminder of the apogee of the Islamic Empire.

The Muslim passion for water greatly influenced floral decors and made it possible to introduce water into architecture and also urban planning. One can even say that the carpet, with its floral exuberance, is the artificial garden of the poor, bringing as it does the shapes and colors of nature into the penumbra of the home.

Fortresses. Arab military architecture is a remarkable phenomenon. No matter where one goes in Spain, the Maghreb or Asia, one will see huge fortified walls scaling the hills, elegant crenellated ramparts or powerful square towers.

In many cases they confined themselves to merely occupying former Christian strong points: Ukaïdir in Irak, Anmour in Turkey are among the most striking of these citadels scattered about the Empire.

A more interesting and original structure is the *ribat,* a sort of fortified monastery

which is to be seen everywhere, from Morocco to Iran. Soldier-monks defended both frontiers and strategic points—as well as their faith—from these structures. They constituted a sort of religious, warlike and mystical chivalry, the Templars and the Knights of Malta or Jerusalem.

The *ribats,* which were always sober and even austere, were supremely elegant on account of the perfection of their volume and proportions, and the stark impression of power which they created.

Decoration

Islam's greatest success of all was in the field of decoration; there it displayed its acute sense of colors, doubtless a reaction to the monotonous ochre tones of the desert all around.

One reason for the exceptional dissemination of its ornamental technique was the low cost of craftsmanship: the labor of the artist did not count at all in the price of the finished work, which was really worth only the cost of the raw materials used.

For this reason even the poor and the lower classes, who had a keen sense of beauty and detail, often had their own personal work of art, such as an enameled star, a piece of sculpted stucco or a small painted statue.

Monumental ornamentation. Dazzling in its exuberant profusion and fascinating in the delicacy of its shades of emphasis, this was the triumph of Muslim plastic art.

Originally Islamic buildings were all in perfect sober proportion and quite bare. Using often very modest materials such as bricks, the architects managed to achieve grandiose effects through the harmony of volume and line.

The result was a great homogeneity and a very pure symbiosis between line and matter: the earth was asked to bring the forms into being and was then given the task of decorating them, with arches, molds and reliefs which were always discreet and few in number.

147

From the origins (8th century) to the Seljucids (12th century) both the construction and decoration of buildings were entrusted to brick.

The Mongols (13th century) and particularly the Timurids (15th century) were the first ones to use, timidly at first, polychrome enameled bricks as a means of enhancing architectural volumes; in this they continued the ancient traditions of the Achemenids and the Assyrians.

But the explosion of color was the work of the Sefevids of Iran. Color was evidently a necessity, as a reaction to the monotony of the desert which, thitherto, had given rise only to the use of puddle-clay throughout the Middle East.

The invasion of polychrome techniques occurred in two phases:

First, at the beginning of the dynasty (1502), using the juxtaposition, mosaic-style, of small monochrome tiles, making up a whole decor piece by piece. Despite its artistic and technical merits this method was slow and costly.

When the time came to decorate huge surfaces some other technique had to be found, one faster and less burdensome, but equally spectacular.

This was the work of the artists of the 17th century, who were pressed into action by their impatient kings and their penchant for architectural projects on a gigantic scale.

Use was then made of ceramic tiles, ten inches square in most cases, and about an inch thick, on which part of the design had been pre-drawn, in seven colors. The individual pieces were then assembled and the entire design obtained.

The town of Kashan, on the edge of the desert, already famed for its potters, became famous by specializing in the making of these *haft rangis* (seven-color tiles) which thereafter became known as *kashi*.

The advantage was the simplification of the laying of the tiles and the drop in the cost. Drawbacks included a poorer-quality finish and particularly a less brilliant finish, due to the fact that each color had a different baking temperature. Theoretically the ideal baking temperatures range between 800 and 1,500 degrees Centigrade, whereas the *kashis* were baked uniformly at a mean temperature of 900 degrees. This accounts for the difference between the gloss on certain tints, which may be faded as a result of too much or too little heat. Hence the dull, faded appearance of certain late decors.

The motifs, which had traditionally been geometric, began to include floral figures (which were prevalent at the Mongol court of Herat) and stylized calligraphy, closely interwoven with the decor.

The advantage of these floral compositions was that they allowed a more supple type of ornamentation, more curved, which blended perfectly with the convex surfaces by means of the twisted arabesques of the motifs.

As for the colors, while there were theoretically seven in the kashis, two of these actually were dominant: green and blue had the value of a talisman and a symbol, being the colors of Islam.

Another characteristic of the varnished Iranian polychrome decor was the discovery, beneath apparent symmetry, of an astonishing diversity. Even though the ornamental structures were similar in any given building, the details were always different: the cartouches and the flowers may be similar, but not identical. The themes are similar but not repeated. This variety in symmetry and in the unity of the whole is the supreme refinement of that decorative style, which always managed to be renewed and personalized, within an apparently stereotyped and uniform profusion.

Total harmonic perfection in the juxtaposition of tints is another feature of these sumptuous compositions.

The decorative arts

The fashion for placing these colossal wall-coverings of varnished ceramics on monuments was paralleled by the contributions of every single type of material and craftsmanship to the decoration of things and interiors, whether public, private or religious.

Sculpture and painting: Semitic traditions had turned away from sculpture and painting, and the Koran frowned on the representation in art of human or animal figures, as a manifestation of pagan idolatry.

For the theologians of Islam such images were a blasphemous usurpation of the creative power which belonged exclusively to God, because it lent life to things through images.

Islamic statuary is therefore insignificant. Virtually all that is known is the famous Lions of the Alhambra. Apart from that there are the works that resulted from the highly unusual decision of a rich Egyptian to have sculptures made of all his women, and also some rare statues from the Omayyad period.

That leaves abstract ornamental sculpture, in stone or stucco, which is responsible for the hard lace patterns which decorate so many mihrabs.

On the other hand, the peoples which adopted Islam later, like the Mongols and the Persians, took less notice of the dogmatic prohibitions, and even painted frescoes. Some of them are historical, depicting battles, royal encounters, banquet scenes or courtly celebrations; while others are domestic, and deal with love, flowers and poetry.

Much use was made in such works of gilded and bright colors, in keeping with the style and the process used in the miniatures.

Art of the object. It was only normal that it should reach such a level of perfection and quality in such a refined society. And *objets d'art* were to be found in the homes

of people throughout society: enameled and metallized pottery; tanned, dyed, glossy or incrusted leather; wood inlaid in gold or ivory or painted; glass shaped into staned glass windows or molded as glass past with colored inclusions; copper, whether chiseled, hammered, or inlaid with gold or silver thread; finely worked ivory; hard stones set in precious metals. All in all a dazzling fairy-like ornamentation in day-to-day objects.

Ceramics, however, continued to be the preferred material because of the ease with which it lends itself to brilliant coloring. Yet one of the characteristics of the art of the Islamic craftsman was his fondness for trying out the same ornamental technique on different materials, with varying results.

Another point to be noted is that, although the general guidelines followed by Islamic artists were identical, there are great differences from one region to the next, sometimes from one town to the next. The apparent homogeneity is due to the absence of a gap between the sacred and the profane, as this meant that art in general was made uniform, under the banner of Islam.

Calligraphy, illumination and miniatures

Monumental calligraphy made from bricks laid in relief or of enamelled ceramic characters reproduces extracts from the Koran or the ninety names of Allah, which would, on their own, suffice to cover an entire façade.

Arabic characters, whether archaic (Kufic) or modern can be stylized to weave the most ornamental of turquoise blue garlands around domes and minarets.

This art used to be so popular that certain artists worked at it exclusively, deriving great honor and fame: the most celebrated of them were Ali Rezza Abbassi and

Mir Amad, *protégés* of Shah Abbas, who vied with each other to adorn the buildings of Isfahan in the 17th century.

The art of illumination, which was really calligraphy on the scale of whole books, was so much in vogue that it quickly crossed the boundaries of Islam and influenced the style of the famous books of hours in the Middle Ages in Europe.

The ornamentation of manuscripts is in fact an oriental invention and speciality particularly rooted in the Turko-Uranian region.

Pious books were adorned with religious calligraphy, and others with decorative arabesques, sometimes with painted scenes or polychrome geometric motifs.

Much painstaking research also went into binding: thick leathers were used, engraved or inlaid with precious stones or metals.

As for the miniatures, they are perhaps the most typical manifestation of the oriental sensitivity to color, shapes and movement.

This art, which was specially highly developed in Iran and Turkey, reached its zenith between the 15th and 17th centuries, but it still survives today, faithful to its themes and its traditional techniques.

One finds the same unchanging themes: polo games (this being the national sport of the Sassanids); charges of mounted warriors under the banner of Allah; savage hand-to-hand fighting in the midst of cavalry battles; love scenes in the orchards in bloom; or reproductions of daily life in the oases with their low-roofed houses.

There is much that is conventional and stereotyped in these naive images, but also the freshness of an ineffable poetry, bathed with charm.

Music

The music of Islam was born of the assimilation, against a background of ancient Scythian and Sassanid sources, of Chinese and Hindu music. This mixture of influences was catalyzed by the temperament peculiar to the countries of Islam, and personalized in each region.

The instruments were not original: flute, both transverse and straight; harp; lute; trumpets of various sorts; drums and tambourines to mark the rhythm; and even an ancestor of the piano, the *qunum*.

Learned music is an art intended to provide intellectual entertainment. Often associated with traditional dances and the recitation of poems at refined courtly parties given by the kings or nobles.

At the other end of the scale, popular music was heard at all the ceremonies of traditional Muslim life: births, marriages, circumcisions. It was almost always military, relying heavily on the sound of the trumpet and of drums carried by camels.

Barely tolerated by Mohammed and the Islam of the first caliphs, music was viewed with suspicion as potentially dangerous and subversive because of its "softening" power, while dancing was regarded as outright depraved eroticism and banned accordingly.

Yet it was the Prophet himself who had arranged the melody of the call to prayer, while certain sects, such as the Whirling Dervishes used and still use its power of mystical exaltation during their ritual ceremonies.

Regardless of the instruments used or the merits of the performers, oriental music is characterised by a poverty of musical phrase, and a sad, poignant monotony; yet it exudes a nostalgic and fascinating charm, precisely because it corresponds to exactly to the Bedouin soul, which is both fatalistic and enthusiastic, gruff and mystical, melancholic and passionate.

These interminable recitatives made it possible to escape more easily from the arid world of day-to-day life and dream of the paradise of Allah, where the sand is golden, the cavalry charges always victorious and the gardens always balmy.

6. THE ISLAMIC FAITH

Before Mohammed the Bedouins had had only a faint religious sense. Admittedly they had all the superstitions of fetishist pagans, but this was a matter for their beliefs and themselves, and was subject to no ecclesiastical structure.

As the Prophet launched himself into his task of disseminating Islam, the Middle East was already being pulled in opposite directions by the other two great revealed religions, Judaism and Christianity.

Mohammed knew both of them and respected them. The Islam which he preached was nothing more than the adaptation of the same monotheistic principle to his own race.

Mohammed did not view himself as God or as an emanation of God: he was only an intermediary, a worker in that new faith which Allah had just revealed to him—a prolongation of Abraham in the Arab ethnic stock.

Moreover, he recognized that he had the same roots as the two other monotheistic religions. It was reform rather than competition that he had in mind, so as to find the best way of adapting the same religious principles to his people.

This explains why the three religions originally had so much in common: all three are revealed, all three share the same origins and recognize the same patriarchs: Noah, Moses and Abraham.

Muslim mythology has many episodes in common with the Judeo-Christian legend: Noah, the Flood, the Last Judgment, etc.

Mohammed also honored and respected Christ, whom he recognized as a Prophet, the only difference being that his birth, which was regarded as divine and miraculous, was situated by Islamic mythology in a small oasis in the desert!

There is thus no opposition between Islam and the Judeo-Christian faith; they rather succeed and complement each other.

In each religion a careful distinction must be made between faith, religion and theocracy: faith is a private matter for men; religion is the whole body of disciplinary and hierarchic rules established by the clergy for the use of that faith; and theocracy is the art of transforming the force of belief into political power wielded in the name of God.

For Mohammed faith merged with religion and with the state. The political concern which created Arabism side by side with Islam came into being only at a later stage. To begin with everything was mixed: Allah was in life of each individual, since he was the homeland of all.

After Mohammed's death, during the historical caliphate, there was not always a separation between Arabism and Islam, which overlapped completely.

The faith advanced throughout the world on the tip of the lances and the pounding of the camel's hoofs of the Bedouin.

But when the territorial expansion of the Arabs could no longer keep up with the fantastic dissemination of their religion, which had been adopted enthusiastically by the conquered peoples, the super-position of Islam and the Arab state ceased to be.

The Omayyads were the first to separate religion and politics, while at the same time preserving a harmonious balance between mysticism and pragmatism.

The Abassids, on the other hand, were so decadent that they soon lost control of both.

Paradoxically, however, this was the point of departure of a fantastic dissemination of Islam, which was merged this time not with a state or a body of policy, but with an exceptional civilization.

Just as Judeo-Christian believers have the Bible, Muslims have the Koran, the Arabic name of which means 'the reading'.

This book, being the whole body of revelations made by God to his Prophet,

A picture on ceramic of the center of Mecca. Right: some lines of the Prophet's handwriting; bottom: the imprint of one of the Prophet's feet.

who had been chosen as an intermediary to transmit the divine directives to the Bedouin people, is therefore *the* Islamic 'reading' *par excellence*.

These revealed instructions nurtured the preaching of Mohammed and their transmission was entirely oral. Only a few faithful disciples recorded them in writing, but loosely and unsystematically.

Abu Bakr, then Omar, the first caliphs, had tried in 638 to compile these scattered notes which constituted the sole written trace of Mohammed's preaching. But it was the glory of Othman, the third Caliph that he was able to reconstitute and arrange in order all the material of the revelations in one sacred book, the Koran, the first work in the Arabic language which was published and disseminated throughout the Islamic Empire, and soon, from 650 onwards, throughout the world.

Being divinely inspired, the text is thus essentially undisputable in its form and infallible in its spirit.

The Koran

This work is—chronologically—the last expression of the word of God for believers, since he had previously manifested himself in the Judeo-Christian revelations.

As the Koran is the ultimate divine teaching, it represents both the dogma and the thinking of Islam, dictated by Allah himself. They are to be found all along the *Suras* (Arabic name for the chapters of the holy book). The version of Othman consists of six thousand two hundred and twenty-six verses, arranged in one hundred and fourteen *suras*.

Originally many of the chapters led to protests from former companions of the Prophet. The Shiites were particularly vociferous, claiming that verses devoted

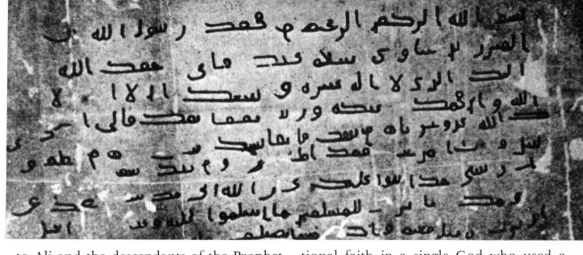

to Ali and the descendants of the Prophet were deleted or modified on the orders of Othman himself, for obvious political reasons.

The basic structure of the work can be described schematically in a few essential ideas. The highest virtue is absolute submission to God; belief in God and the Prophets is imperative, total and undisputable; the dogma of the revelation of Islam is inviolate: it is God himself who dictated the holy book; the cult of the angels is part of the Muslim faith: Michael, the executor of the divine instructions, Usrafil the player of the trumpet of the Last Judgment, Israfil, archangel of death, and in particular Gabriel (Djebrail), the intermediary between God and men, who transmitted the word of Allah to Mohammed.

The practical applications of these dogmas gave rise to a highly ritual religion without much ceremonial, demanding without being oppressive, and mystical but also human.

Allah, despite his transcendental status, is actually close to man; and Islam, despite its scrupulous dogmatism, is a part of the daily life of each Muslim, impregnating him and shaping him within his personality.

Faith and Prayer

The fundamental profession of faith which recurs like a *leit-motiv,* instilling into the minds of the faithful the notion that "Allah alone is great, God alone is God, and Mohammed is his Prophet", is based on a series of imperative obligations of the believer, the Five Pillars of the Moslem faith: faith, prayer, alms, fasting and the pilgrimage to Mecca.

Faith: a total, exclusive, and uncondi-tional faith in a single God who used a Prophet, Mohammed, to reveal himself to men.

Prayer: a creation of Mohammed. It is imperative, but may take place anywhere, even on the battlefield, and does not need the framework of the mosque.

It must be preceded by ritual ablutions. Though intended to clean the body, like any normal set of hygienic rules, they also have a symbolic role: the 'legal purity' needed before one is presented to one's God.

In the absence of water—as is frequently the case in Islamic countries—sand can be used. First the feet are cleansed, then the hands and finally the face.

Prayer is a private matter between Allah and each believer: five times each day the individual must show himself to his

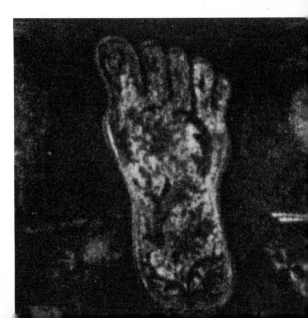

Creator: one hour before sunrise; at noon; in the middle of the afternoon, at about five o'clock; one hour before, and lastly one hour after, the setting of the sun.

This periodicity, this rhythm, is designed to occupy the daily life of the believer and make sure that he does not forget his God.

In the small villages, the *muezzin*—a sort of Islamic sacristan, unpaid and not professional—climbs each time to the minaret and chants the call to prayer, praising Allah and his Prophet.

In the towns he has been replaced by a loudspeaker; strained, nasal tones carry his exhortation out over the teeming or sleeping city.

This call of the muezzin, the *Azar,* was created by Mohammed, even in its musical aspects. The type of chant was left to the choice of the singer, using as a general rule the traditional ancestral themes of the region.

The Islamic chant, which is a kind of transposition of the Christian bell or the Jewish horn, provides precisely the kind of mystical tremor which is designed to induce a state of receptivity in the believer.

A good Muslim devotes two hours a day

to his compulsory prayers, not counting those which he may choose to add personally, nor his readings of the Koran.

The ritual involves, in succession, the washing of the hands before being presented to God, and then prostration before the Divinity, forehead touching the ground, facing Mecca, which is the center of the Islamic world.

Often a small tablet of baked clay, supposed to have come from the Holy City, is placed on the prayer mat and kissed symbolically at each genuflexion.

No other religion keeps up this constant needling pressure which brings man face to face with his God five times a day.

The fact that the mosques are often not very full is of no significance; Muslims pray wherever they happen to be, a truck driver on the road, a sailor on his boat, a camel driver in the desert, and a craftsmen in his shop.

Every Friday, however, a collective prayer takes place in the Great Mosque, under the spiritual direction of an imam, an ulema or a mollah.

Islam has no priests in the Christian sense of the term, since there is no celebration, sacrament or ceremony held in the mosque. The mollahs, imams and ayatol-

Left: a muezzin, from the top of a minaret, summons the faithful to prayer.
Below: holy man preaching in a mosque, Samarkand.

lahs are simply members of the Islamic clergy, each occupying a place in the hierarchy. Just like the ulemas, who are theologians and doctors of the faith, they confine themselves to reading and commenting on the Koran.

Meetings in the mosque are therefore nothing more than the fraternal communion of the believers of all classes, brought together in the veneration of their common God: each individual is alone, and at the same time each one can see all the others in the assembly. Unlike the church, the mosque is not a holy or consecrated place; it is merely a meeting place for the faithful.

Here we find, therefore, the two main features of Islam: the permanent solitude of man before God, and, at the same time, his collective communion with his brothers: individualism and fraternity being the two keys, less contradictory than complementary, of the Muslim world.

The interior of the famous El-Azhar mosque, Cairo.

Alms, fasting, the pilgrimage to Mecca

Legal alms. Having been crucial at the beginning for the success of the conquest, and then the expansion of the Islamic faith and of Muslim Arab civilization, the *Zakat* is still in force. This compulsory tithe or sacred charity continues to sustain the religious hierarchies, now having the effect of consolidating the theocratic powers than of upholding the faith.

The amounts involved are sometimes considerable. Among the Shiites of Iran it comes to five per cent of all private transactions carried out by the merchants in the bazaars; this gives the clergy very great economic power.

Fasting. This habit was borrowed from the Jews and the Nestorian Christians; it is less a mortification of the flesh, as has been wrongly said, than a symbolic and voluntary expiation of the sins of the year.

Ramadan, with its forty days of strict fasting, also has a great psychological impact which is also mystical and almost political.

With extremely rare exceptions, for pressing reasons of health, no Muslim fails to abide by the rules of Ramadan. Even the most lukewarm believers do not dare openly challenge tradition, and conform to it.

From sunrise to sunset it is forbidden to take either drink or food, or even to smoke, or have sexual relations.

The vagaries of the Muslim calendar sometimes cause the month of Ramadan to fall in the middle of the summer, thus further aggravating the real difficulties of compliance. Only travelers who have set before dawn on a long desert journey are authorized to drink a little water during the day.

In the early years of Islam there were some fanatics who did not even swallow their own saliva, choosing to spit it out instead!

On the other hand, as soon as sunset comes, a night of merrymaking often makes up for so much heroism, thus wiping out the mystical benefits and the purifying virtues of fasting. Although in the villages the rite of Ramadan is still fully respected, in the towns it is usually expressed in summary form by a ban on eating and drinking in public during the first and last days of the month.

This may seem to be a contradiction of Mohammed's preaching against asceticism; he argued that Allah would ask nothing unpleasant or difficult of his people.

The pilgrimage to Mecca. The *Kajj,* as it was called, used to be practised long before Islam. It was consecrated by Mohammed, who made it into the crowning event of one's religious and social life, as well as a fraternal contact symbolizing the unity of the Muslim world.

It was in the middle of winter, for obvious climatic reasons, that the official pilgrimage took place. But it could be done at any time of the year.

The journey known as *Unra* was originally a part of the pilgrimage.

One must admit that it was not simple, over hundreds or thousands of miles of trails, which in those days must have been deadly and endless.

Along the way the caravanserais offered the pilgrim the pleasures of their hospitality, and a few military bands helped bolster, if necessary, their flagging courage.

Once they had reached the Holy City, the pilgrims had themselves shaved; then they solemnly put on a special cloak made of two pieces of seamless white fabric. Then they recited a special prayer, the *tabliya,* which dedicated their journey and their pilgrimage to God.

Then they joined the crowd of other believers and performed a ritual and compulsory circuit, with unchanging stages.

The Kaaba, where they kissed the black stone before walking seven times around the building, while reciting formulas in praise of Allah.

158

Arafa, a town some 10 miles (three hours' walk) from Mecca, where, at the end of the afternoon, they climbed a small hill to await the sunset with dozens of thousands of pilgrims, all standing, facing God, exhorted by the suras of the Koran, chanted in chorus.

They would then come back down at nightfall, after the last evening prayer. Deeply impressed and imbued with faith they slept at Mozdalkfa, the closest village, often on the bare ground, under the night sky.

The next day they went to Nina, between Mecca and Arafa, where they threw stones symbolically at a rock which represented Satan and his temptations.

There, each pilgrim had to offer the sacrifice of one goat, one sheep or one camel, depending on what he could afford, thus transforming the mystical ceremony into a bloody scene of carnage. When cooked, the meat was used partly to feed the pilgrims, and partly for distribution to the poor.

Many of them used to go on to Medina, to meditate on the Prophet's tomb.

The pilgrims' circuit then ended. They would go around the Kaaba another seven times, don their normal clothes and leave the town, keeping within their souls an unforgettable memory of their *kajj* and henceforth having a glorious title which would follow them about for the rest of their lives.

After such a pilgrimage they had to be called *kajji,* or *Hafj,* to honor their great devotion, which would bring them the indulgence of Allah on the day of the Last Judgment.

All those who could do so returned home via Jerusalem, the other great Holy City of Islam, to venerate the memory of Abraham, which was common to the revealed religions.

There were, and there still are, five hundred thousand pilgrims each year on the great pilgrimage to Mecca, the ritual of which has not changed.

As in the other great religions, the faith of the pilgrims was exploited by hordes of merchants selling souvenirs and other junk, by pickpockets and other parasites of the sort which plague any large gathering of people.

In a matter of a few days a pilgrim could part with a whole year's earnings. Quite clearly this immense confluence of people was mainly intended to develop the sense of Muslim fraternity, by staging a colossal demonstration of its mystical, even fanatical unity, based on the Koran and Allah.

Moreover, all pilgrims who had been to Mecca came back convinced that they had seen the center of the world. They had also become aware, in the midst of the cosmopolitan mixing of races around the Kaaba, of the universal power of the Islamic faith. There was in this mass manifestation, besides its religious significance, a clear political meaning. The votive procession at Persepolis—much in the same way—was the cement of the unity of ancient Persia.

Minor requirements

Besides the five Pillars of the Faith there was a series of minor requirements which had only a secondary and often utilitarian, hygienic or social value.

A ban on eating the flesh of the pig, since that animal was symbolic of impurity; this ban may also have been influenced by the fact that pork can give humans the parasite known as tenia.

A ban on eating dead animals—again officially because of their impurity and the blood they contained, but also, doubtless, for obvious reasons of hygiene.

A ban on drinking wine or alcohol: the damage drinking could cause to the health of both individuals and society being even more catastrophic in such hot climates.

Drunkenness, by denying man his self-control and awareness, made him unworthy of God and an easy prey for Satan.

Apart from the pilgrimage to Mecca and Ramadan, there were other festivals which reunited the believers in paroxysms of faith: the feast of the Prophet's birthday; the feast of the month of Shaaban, devoted to the destiny of man; the commemoration of the sacrifice of Abraham, which was very solemnly celebrated on the last four days of the last month of the year: on this occasion, each family ritually sacrificed a lamb, while the ordinary people, clad in their finest clothes, paraded around the gaily decorated streets, pausing to pray in the illuminated mosque.

Once stripped of the hocus-pocus of their rites and myths and of political miscalculations, the Muslim legend and ethics may be described schematically as follows:

Allah is the sole and unique God. He has ninety-nine different names—a fact which, apart from anything else, provided considerable material for artistic calligraphy.

He revealed his existence and his precepts successively to Abraham, Moses, Christ and Mohammed, the last of whom was the depositary of the latest vision of the same belief. It is important to note how the original identity of the monotheist faith led to an insurmountably detailed dynastic and theological opposition.

Nobody may question the dogmas. Faith is the highest moral value; and the fundamental sins are committed more against the spirit than against the flesh, which is the beginning of heresy and reactionary inquisition.

Since Mohammed left many equivocal or obscure points, it was the theological interpretation of the *ulemas,* or Doctors of the Faith, which finally provided a answer to them through the *Sunna,* or science of interpretation of the Koran. It is interesting to note that this word gave rise to the adjective *Sunnite,* applied to Muslim orthodoxy.

The center of Muslim religious life is the heart of the faithful and the mosque,

the house for meetings, contacts and prayers concerning God.

The main precepts of the Koran are charity, hospitality, fidelity to one's word, and protection of widows and orphans. Therefore, were it not for the Law of Retaliation, a barbarous form of legalized vengeance in keeping with the vindictiveness of the Arab character, which was included as a final concession to pre-Islamic custom—the Koran would have been just like a copy of the Gospels. After all, although Islam is a religion of love, it is also a religion of conquest, and more warlike than contemplative; this is doubtless due to the underlying personality of the men to whom it was addressed.

Orientals, being meditative, have a religion of thought; whereas the hypercivilized Westerner has a religion of spectacle; Arabs, being more instinctive and rougher, have a religion of action.

All of them are similar in that they tend towards the elevation of man and seek to develop his personal thoughts and mystical awareness.

In this sense Islam is a harmonious but contradictory mixture between the spirituality of an undisputable faith, the dogmatic precepts of a religion which is as pragmatic and utilitarian as it is mystic and transcendental and the political needs of a form of power which is permanently tempted in the direction of theocracy.

The Muslim sects

All of them claimed to derive from Mohammed and Allah and are thus, from that point of view, purist and intransigent. They therefore came into being only as a reaction against a religious softening, and are designed to heighten the fanaticism of the faithful in order to achieve the purest possible Islam.

This phenomenon is certainly evidence of the astonishing vitality of this religion, which refused to get bogged down in routine and sought, instead, an unbroken resurgence of the spirit of the Prophet, and movement towards a perfection which, though never attained, was always pursued.

Each sect is a veritable religious guild seeking salvation through a rigorous application of the Koran.

The Koran is essentially inviolate, demanding and omnipotent.

When muslim civilization becomes ensnared in luxury and comfort, the source of decadence, a sudden jolt is needed on the part of Islam as a whole in order to sublimate it and renew its mission for the conquest of souls. The periodic revival of Islam is the role of the more or less marginal sects.

The Puritans:

The Kharijites, who emerged from the ranks of the Companions of Ali on the death of the Prophet, began by rejecting the control of the Omayyads, the last of the converts, over 'their' religion. These grim, rebellious warriors used military force to fight what they regarded as a revolutionary deviation and religious treason.

The Shiites:

This sect, which was more theoretically inclined, confined itself to disputing the spiritual authority of the elected caliphs. They were intransigent orthodox believers who recognized only the family line of the Prophet himself (Fatima, his daughter; Ali, his son-in-law; and Hussein, his grandson). This was more a problem of individuals

than of religious style. In fact they were also attacked by the Kharijites as being decadent in respect of the Prophet's spirit, just like the Omayyads.

For the Shiites, their imam is more than a holy man, he is the depositary of a portion of hereditary divinity. For them the first imam was Ali and the second Hussein. They thus recognize twelve dynastic imams. Generally speaking, all Arabs, the Turks and remote Muslims (Africa, Asia) are Sunnites (i.e., faithful to the elected caliphate), while the Iranians and some Irakis are Shiites, that is to say, faithful to the dynasty of the imams.

The Ismaelians:

This sect was created in Cairo to give support to the dynastic claims of the families which were directly descended from the Prophet. They followed the Shiites as far the sixth imam, and then went their own way.

Jafarsadeq, the sixth imam, chose to make his youngest son the heir to his spiritual patrimony, to the detriment of his eldest son, Ismael.

Since that time, as far as the Ismaelians are concerned, the only legitimate imams have been Ismael and his descendants.

Starting in the 11th century, this opposition, which had originally been a mere quarrel over legitimacy, soon became aggressive and destructive, particularly in Iran.

The sect of the Ismaelians of Iran was founded in about 1080 by Hassan-ben-Sabbah, who had been born in Rey in about 1040; he had studied philosophy and theology at Nishabour with Omar Khayyam, the poet-philosopher, and Nizan-al-Molk, who became the grand vizir of three successive sultans.

Hassan-ben-Sabbah caused the objectives of the Iranian branch to deviate by making it more fanatical and imposing on it the strait-jacket of strict hierarchic discipline, in order to turn it into an instrument of power rather than of the faith.

The structure of the sect was as follows:

At the top, the *rais,* a small number of chiefs who were kept abreast of all the secrets, of the 'Order', and whose aim was the destruction of the existing kingdoms and centers of power.

Under their orders, the *refiks,* who were something approaching 'companions', were given the job of propagating the sectarian faith and fanaticising the people, while remaining unaware of their masters' true political plans.

At the base, the *fedavis,* who were mere instruments, crammed with mystical sentiment and fanaticism, were used for the dirty work—murders, violence and assassination—and constituted the sect's means of exerting pressure.

This power of the Ismaelians of Iran gradually increased, thanks to the support of the grand vizir Nizan-al-Molk, who obtained for his comrade Hassan the support of the Seljucid monarchs, viewing this religious crusade as nothing more than commendable zeal to achieve more purity and discipline for the greater glory of Islam.

But when he found that his sect was well established and powerful enough, Hassan-ben-Sabbah withdrew for the rest of his days to his castle at Alamut, and became the legendary Old Man of the Mountain.

From the vantage point of this eyrie, he organized and conducted countless punitive raids and attacks, killing off the powerful men of the kingdom on the pretext of punishing their laxity in religious affairs and morals; in fact, however, he was merely destroying the existing power structure.

His former benefactor and fellow-disciple, the grand vizir Nizan-al-Molk, was, together with Sultan Melek, his first choice victim.

These political assassinations were carried out by *fedavis* who had been transported to paroxysms of mystical fanaticism and were drugged with hashish; this accounts for their name of *Hashishin,* which came into English as *assassin.*

The Old Man of the Mountain died in 1124 in his favorite citadel of Alamut, at the height of his bloodthirsty power. The sect survived his death, further accentuating his terrorist activities, until the coming of the Mongols in 1220. The newcomers organized in 1254 a punitive operation against the Ismaelian citadels, which they razed to the ground mercilessly, thus putting an end to the extraordinary adventure of the sect of the 'Assassins'.

The Druses of Syria are a much more discreet offshoot of this sect.

Sufism:

A Muslim mystic whose name comes from *Suf,* for the woolen robe worn by the first faithful of Islam and from *Safa,* purity.

Adepts of Suffims claim to reach God merely through love and contemplative introspection.

It was the main channel through which Hindu influences entered Islam.

Its leader, Al-Kallaj was persecuted by orthodox Muslims and executed in 927. This dissident spiritual movement continued, however, by seeking a compromise between the exacerbated purity of the Sufis and the traditional dogma; from the 15th century onwards they moved more and more towards the confraternities of Dervishes. Some still remain in Afghanistan, particularly at Herat, where they represent the very Hindu form of contemplative spirituality in Islam.

The Dervishes:

This is a Persian word meaning 'beggar'; its applies to the mystics, ascetics and fanatics, who emanated from Sufism and represented the austere and unrelenting face of Islam. Made up for the most part of lay persons and a minority of monks, it has taken Islam towards greater profundity

Below: the Kaaba, at Mecca. Right: inscriptions on a wall in the house of an Egyptian Muslim who has made the traditional pilgrimage to Mecca. Following pages: frontispiece of an 18th-century Koran now in the Mosque of the Omayyads, Damascus; miniature showing Mohammed surrounded by disciples; bottom: detail of a 10th-century Koran (Teheran).

and a more intransigent interpretation of the Koran; its members even make Mohammed say more than he actually said.

Having more or less the same structure as Hinduism, with masters, disciples and sympathizers, they prospered mainly in Cairo, Iran and Turkey. It is curious to note that here again that those more fiercely opposed to an Islam wedded to routine were the belated converts, non-Arabs, trying to be 'more papist than the Pope'.

The best known and most spectacular of their manifestations are their religious displays of collective fanatical exaltation. For them, control by sheer willpower over breathing, pain and the entire body was more important than meditation.

The purpose was to achieve the transcendental domination of the body by sublimated spirituality, bringing man face to face with God, without material or physiological interference of any sort. This was a liberation of the human being, who was thus released from the dross of earthly things and enabled to float towards heaven.

The Shrieking Dervishes, or Shadhiliyah, founded in the 12th century in Egypt and Iran required their physical exertions—whirling, piercing of the flesh and shouting—to temporarily do away with human awareness in order to achieve mystical ecstasy. Though officially suppressed in 1925 they still continue to function, more or less clandestinely.

The Whirling Dervishes (or Mewlewis) were founded at Konya, in Turkey, by Djabol-ed-din-Roumi in the 13th century.

They attain ecstasy by the empirical use of cerebral anoxia obtained through the centrifugal movement of whirling.

The use of music, a subdued somber recitative very similar to Gregorian chant, does much to induce the state necessary for ecstasy.

The Dervishes, who were ascetics, used to live in monasteries or *tekes,* comparable to those of Christian monks.

Squeezed between political pressures and the weight of religious orthodoxy, the Dervishes are now fast disappearing.

Their original monastery at Konya is turning more and more into a place to visit on the tourist circuit, where records are sold and people pay an entrance fee to watch the ritual dance performed by the last monks of Islam, who whirl, endlessly in an atmosphere which has a higher content of folklore than of mysticism.

The Wahhabites:

These are the supporters of a reform advocated in the 18th century by Mohammed-ibn-Abd-el-Wahhab a Bedouin from a tribe of Nedj, who called for a return to a purer Islam and a traditional view of the Koran.

They rejected the personality cult surrounding the saints and the Prophet. Returning to a simple and frugal life they banned even singing, dancing, games, music and tobacco.

سورة البقرة است

بسم الله الرحمن الرحيم
الم ذلك الكتاب لا ريب فيه
هدى للمتقين الذين يؤمنون
بالغيب ويقيمون الصلوة ومما
رزقناهم ينفقون والذين
يؤمنون بما أنزل اليك وما أنزل
من قبلك وبالآخرة هم يوقنون

وثمانون
ومائتان آية مدنية

الرحمن الرحيم
مالك يوم الدين
نستعين
عليهم
ولا الضالين

Wahhab was so strict that he was expelled from his tribe and sought refuge in the small oasis of Nedj where Ibn-Seoud had also been exiled.

His ideas of sober and rigorous purity, in opposition to an Islam which was fast collapsing in the midst of corruption, progress and Westernization, pleased the future king, who protected him and made him his son-in-law. From the throne of Arabia, Ibn-Seoud imposed Wahhab as the spiritual master of the kingdom.

This sect, which is the most recent of all, has become the most powerful in Islam, of which it represents only the most intact original aspect. It is a kind of rigorous Muslim Protestantism.

Actually all the sects which emanated from Mohammed's Islam have been designed exclusively to move close to God and to be faithful to the Prophet.

Periodiccally they have served as a call for a more dynamic and pure Islam, warning against the debilitating temptations of progress, civilization and Westernization.

This is why these sects tolerate each other so well; there is no Muslim Inquisition, because there is no fundamental dogmatic opposition; theirs is a never-ending competition to achieve the purest and most total Islam.

And in all of this it is life, and the way one lives it, in honor and rigor, that counts. Death has no importance, and no place in these unrelenting efforts to achieve fuller submission to God.

This is because the Muslim believer has total confidence in his faith and does not fear death: the main thing is to live in keeping with the demands of the Prophet; one can be in no doubt: the paradise of Allah will welcome his virtuous fighters.

PERIODS	ARAB WORLD	
PRE-ISLAMIC ANTIQUITY (From the second millenium BC to 570 AD)	500 BC to 500 AD Pre-Islamic Arab civilization in Saudi Arabia	19 19 19 19 11 9 8 7 7 6 6 5 5 5 4 4 336-8 264-1 58- — 2 9 2 4 435-4 481-5
LIFE OF MOHAMMED (570-632)	570-632 Life of Mohammed 610 First preaching at Mecca 622 Hegira: visit to Medina	6 6
THE HISTORIC LEGITIMATE CALIPHATE (632-661)	632-634 Abu Bakr 634-649 Omar 636 Islamic victory over Heraclius of Byzantium at Yarmuk 637 Islamic victory over the Persians at Radesiyya 638 Jerusalem and Antioch taken by the Arabs 642 Alexandria taken by the Arabs Victory of Nehavend over the Persians 644-656 Othman 647 Beginning of the invasion of North Africa 656-661 Ali 661 Overthrow of Ali Beginning of the schism of Islam	629-6 632-6 6

REST OF THE WORLD		CIVILIZATION
	BC	
irst Hittite empire	1755	Code of Hammurabi in Mesopotamia
irst Assyrian empire		
aptivity of the Jews in Egypt	1500-1300	Mycenean and Cretan masterpieces
eign of Ramses II in Egypt		
Iebuchadnezzar, king of Babylon		
olomon, king of Israel, in Jerusalem	900	Temple of Solomon in Jerusalem
oundation of Carthage	776	Foundation of Olympic Games
oundation of Rome		
he Etruscans in Italy		
shurbanipal, king of Assyria		
oundation of Marseille by the Phoceans		
onfucius		
yrus the Great, king of Persia		
arius, king of Persia	470-430	Socrates
eonidas at Thermopylae	430-350	Xenophon
ictory of Themistocles at Salamis	428-347	Plato
lexander the Great, king of Macedonia	287-212	Archimedes
unic Wars between Rome and Carthage	200	Venus of Milo
Var in Gaul: Cesar-Vercingetorix	48	Burning of the library of Alexandria
	AD	
eigns of the great Roman emperors	44 BC to 30 AD?	Life of Christ
wasion of Gaul by the Franks	6	Buddhism in China
wading Barbarians cross the Rhine	45-64	Travels of St Paul
ttila, king of the Huns	64	Burning of Rome. Persecution of Christians
lovis, king of the Franks		
	397-426	Coming of St Augustine
rusalem taken by the Persians		
gobert, king of the Franks	538-593	Gregory of Tours
i Zong, emperor of China		
zdegard III, last king of Sassanid Persia		
sigoth monarchy		

PERIODS	ARAB WORLD	
THE OMAYYADS (661-750) **CENTRALIZED POWER OF ISLAM**	670 Foundation of Kairouan 698 Carthage taken by the forces of Islam 710-713 Conquest of India 711-714 Conquest of Spain 713 Conquest of India halted at Multan, in the Punjab 732 Expansion in Europe halted Charles Martel at Poitiers	
THE ABASSIDS (750-1258) **AND "DIASPORA" OF THE LOCAL ARAB DYNASTIES**	754-775 Al Mansur, Caliphate of Baghdad 786-809 Harun-al-Rashid 813-833 Al-Mamun 825 Occupation of Crete by Islamic forces 827-902 Landings in Sicily; conquest of the island 756-929 Omayyad Emirate of Spain founded by Abd-al-Rahman 786-974 Idrisid Dynasty in Morocco 909-923 Fatimid Dynasty in Maghreb, then in Egypt (foundation of Cairo in 969) 929-1031 Dissident Omayyad Caliphate in Cordoba 973-1171 Fatimid Caliphate in Egypt 962-1186 Turkish Dynasty of the Rhaznevids 1062 Foundation of Marrakesh by the Almoravids 1063-1085 Seljucid invasion and expansion in Turkey 1125 The Almahads established in Morocco, then throughout Spain (1172) 1171 Saladin overthrows the Fatimid Caliphate of Egypt, then founds the Ayyubid Caliphate of Egypt and Syria (1170-1250)	757-7 76 81 840-8 877-8 920-100 9 9 9 100 100 100 11 11 11 11 11 12 1226-12 12
ISLAMIC TERRITORIES GOVERNED BY NON-ARAB MUSLIM DYNASTIES	1250-1798 The Mameluks in Egypt and Syria 1299-1922 The Ottomans in Turkey, then in the Balkans, Irak and Egypt	12 14 17

REST OF THE WORLD	CIVILIZATION	
	670-675	Great mosque of Kairouan
	683-691	Great mosque of Omar, Jerusalem
	705	Great mosque of Damascus
ntificate of St Paul I.	760	Great mosque of Baghdad
arlemagne, king of the Franks	773	Arabic numerals
st attack by Danish Vikings in En	830	Foundation of center for Arabic translation at Baghdad
arles the Bald, king of France	881	Foundation of the temple of Angkor
st Khmer Dynasty of Angkor	932-1020	Ferdawsi, Persian poet
e Toltecs of Mexico	960	Great mosque of Cordova
rwegian Vikings discover Greenland	975	Abbey of Cluny
gues Capet	980-1037	Avicenna, Arab philosopher-doctor
bert the Pious	1004	Monastery of Mount Athos
ilization of Tihuanaco	c. 1050	Frist printed characters in China
st Crusade	1215	Magna Carta
usalem taken by the Crusaders		
arles VII, king of France		
ond Crusade		
derick Barbarossa, Germanic emperor		
enor of Aquitaine marries Henry Plantagenet		
ird Crusade		
ongol invasion in Middle East and China		
nt Louis		
enth Crusade (Saint Louis)		
ghth Crusade	1265-1321	Dante
ath of Saint Louis in Tunis	c. 1387	Chaucer's *Canterbury Tales*
ll of Constantinople	1450	Gutenberg printing press
claration of Independence	1685-1750	Johann Sebastian Bach
	1770	Births of Wordsworth, Beethoven

PERIODS	ARAB WORLD		
EUROPEAN COLONIAL OPERATIONS AGAINST THE ISLAMIC COUNTRIES	1881	French protectorate in Tunisia	1819-19
	1882	British forces occupy Cairo	18
	1906	Conference of Algeciras: France and Spain acquire control over Morocco	18
			1910-19
	1911	German gunboat *Panther* causes international crisis on arrival at Agadir	
			19
MODERN TIMES AND THE RENEWAL OF ISLAM	1926	Ibn Saud, king of the Hejaz and Arabia	19
	1953	Egyptian Republic: Nasser	19
	1956	Independence of Morocco: Mohammed V.	19
	1958	Union of Syria and Egypt	19
	1962	Independence of Algeria	19

REST OF THE WORLD	CIVILIZATION	
ueen Victoria	1847	Charlotte Brontë: *Jane Eyre*
rths of Stalin and Trotsky	1854	Tennyson: *The Charge of the Light Brigade*
e beginning of the "Dreyfus Affair".	1883	Nietzsche
orge V, king of Great Britain	1913	Proust
	1915	Manuel de Falla
eimar Republic		
ichstag fire	1927	Lindberg flies across the Atlantic
ath of Stalin	1928	Fleming discovers penicillin
tionalization of the Suez Canal	1953	First ascent of Everest
rushchov succeeds Bulganin	1957	First *Sputnik*. First earth satellite
ban missile crisis	1962	Firts American orbital flight (John Glenn)

Credits: B.N. Paris: 32 - B.N. Vienne: 24 - Croizat: 2 - 5 - 6 - 9 - 12 - 15 - 18 - 30 - 33 - 37 - 47 - 48 - 52 - 55 - 61 - 62 - 65 - 74 - 76 - 80 - 96 - 102 - 104 - 110 - 111 - 112 - 137 - 143 - 145 - 147 - 176 - Dagli Orti: 10 - 11 - Musée de Chantilly: 40 - 41a - 42b - 44 - 51 - 58 - 59 - 63 - 64 - 66b - 67 - 68b - 69 - 70 - 82 - 86 - 87 - 92 - 93 - 97 - 109 - 113 - 140 - 165 - 168 - 169 - Dulevant/Gemini: 41b - 115 - 149 - 152 - 166 - 167a - Gemini: 17 - 57 - 164 - Musée d'Art et d'Histoire/Genève: 43a - Pizzi/Chiari: end-Papers - 4 - 8 - 45 - 75 - 85 - 88 - 89 - 90 - 91 - 95 - 103 - 114 - 116 - 117 - 133 - 135 - 136a - 138 - 159 - 167b - Rijkmuseum/Amsterdam: 38 - 68a - Aegyptian Tourism Office: 28 - 42a - 66a - Vatican: 150 - Roger-Viollet: 50 - 72 - 73 - 108 - 118 - 119 - 120 - 126 - 134 - 136b - 155 - 162.

Printed in Italy

حجة الاسلام
حاج ملا نحسین هراتی ک

مضی دو المعالی غلام الحسین و فقیه وجیه هو الحسین
بلند قدر بر از جهان غلام حسین که شد فقیه وجیه از محاسن حسین
ولی علی امیر العلا و مسکن شیعة الحسین
ولی اعظم علی عالی قدر که در دوخت جا لاشید در این
صبحة ربیع شوال قد مضی فی اجلن خیال الحسین
صبح چهارم شوال رفت او نمود جای بعالی زین خان حسین
وقت فردا علی النعیم فا رخ وفاق غلام حسین
لایق فایق گرفت فردو بگو وفاق تاریخ دی غلام حسین

تاریخ وفات ۲۵ دیا
۱۳۲۵ شهر